D1366217

THE STRESS FACTOR

THE STRESS FACTOR

THRIVING EMOTIONALLY AND SPIRITUALLY IN THE TURBULENT 90'S

Frank Minirth, M.D., & Paul Meier, M.D.,
of the Minirth-Meier Clinic
Don Hawkins, Th.M.,
Chris Thurman, Ph.D., Richard Flournoy, Ph.D.

NORTHFIELD PUBLISHING
CHICAGO

© 1992 by
NORTHFIELD PUBLISHING
A DIVISION OF MBI
CHICAGO, IL

This volume is a condensed and revised version, with new and original material added, of *How to Beat Burnout,* by Frank Minirth, Don Hawkins, Paul Meier, and Richard Flournoy, © 1986, and *Before Burnout,* by Don Hawkins, Frank Minirth, Paul Meier, and Chris Thurman, © 1990.

ISBN: 1-881273-02-4

3 5 7 9 10 8 6 4 2

Printed in the United States of America

*To our many good friends
from among the obsessive-compulsives
whose lives have impacted and
shaped us to balance our obsessions
by living life one day at a time
with an eye on eternity*

Don Hawkins, Th.M. Director of radio communications for *Rapha, Inc.* and host and executive producer of a nationwide, live, call-in radio program, "Life Perspectives." A veteran conference and seminar speaker, he has nineteen years of pastoral experience.

Frank Minirth, M.D. Cofounder and president of the Minirth-Meier Clinic headquartered in Richardson, Texas. He is cohost of several weekday radio and television programs, including "The Minirth-Meier Clinic," a nationwide, live, call-in radio program. He also serves as adjunct professor of pastoral ministries at Dallas Theological Seminary.

Paul Meier, M.D. Executive vice-president of the Minirth-Meier Clinic in Richardson, Texas, and cohost of the Minirth-Meier radio program. He has written or coauthored numerous self-help books relating to common psychological issues.

Chris Thurman, M.D. Licensed psychologist at the Minirth-Meier Tunnell and Wilson Clinic in Austin, Texas. In addition to his private practice, he serves as a consultant to businessmen in the areas of stress management and assertiveness. He is the author of several books including *The Lies We Believe*.

Richard Flournoy, Ph.D. A licensed psychologist in full-time private practice in the Dallas area. He is the author or coauthor of numerous books.

CONTENTS

ACKNOWLEDGMENTS

The authors would like to gratefully acknowledge those whose contributions helped to make this book possible.

Special thanks goes to a number of people who risked burnout to type and compile the manuscript. Those include Carol Mandt, Teresa Pakiz, Debra Stack, Jim Schneider, and Kathy Short.

Further thanks goes to Marty Williams Anderson for extensive writing and editorial work, which included coordinating the efforts of different authors.

INTRODUCTION

While in north Dallas recently I decided to take advantage of a couple of hours' free time to pay an old friend a visit. I hadn't seen him in several years, but a mutual friend had mentioned his name to me the previous week, and I decided to look him up.

An elevator gently whisked me into the heart of a glass-and-steel skyscraper, and I stepped off into the plush reception area of a major-market radio station. It was quite a contrast to the spartan central Texas studios where Bob had first introduced me to radio broadcasting.

The receptionist smiled and asked, "May I help you?" When I explained that I had dropped by to visit Bob, I was shocked by her response. Her face reacted as if she had been hit. Her voice quivered, and tears came to her eyes. Choking, she whispered, "You haven't heard?"

"What happened?" was all I could reply.

It took her a minute to form the words. "Bob is dead! A little over a year ago. We just couldn't believe it."

Several memories flashed through my mind, like slides in rapid-fire sequence. Bob's pleasant laughter when I threw the wrong switch on my first encounter with a radio control board. Pleasant mornings spent drinking coffee and discussing the ins and outs of radio production. Bob's patience in handling equipment failures. The smile on his face when he told me he had been appointed operations manager of a major Dallas station.

My mind replayed tapes of numerous conversations on subjects ranging from political to spiritual to nonsensical. Still, I couldn't quite grasp the full impact of what I had just been told. After all, Bob was only a few years older than I. The last time I saw him he seemed in prime health. What happened?

Winking back her tears, the receptionist continued. "We really miss Bob. We still can't believe it." She went on to explain that Bob had encountered two major job failures and the breakup of his marriage, all within a short span of time.

I waited for an opportunity to phrase my question. "Did he have an accident? A heart attack?"

I'll never forget her reply: "No," she said, "Bob died of natural causes. Even the doctor said Bob just burned out."

Burnout, a term heard with increasing frequency these days, is a prominent fact of life in the fast-paced and stress-filled final decade of our twentieth century. In gathering material for this book, we discovered that people in all walks of life are experiencing stress and burnout, perhaps as never before. We have found burnout within our own families, our counseling staff, our colleagues, and in the lives of a large proportion of the people with whom we interact. Most of us have experienced some degree of burnout, at least short-term, or we have been close to someone who has. All of us writing this book have experienced significant stress and know what burnout is firsthand.

Except for a few such as Bob, or those who use suicide as a way of escape, most of us do not die from burnout. Eventually we recover to some degree.

Yet many wait too long to counter its effects, or they try dead-end roads to ease the strain. They end up losing their jobs, their health, and sometimes their families. They may never recover from those effects.

That is the bad news.

The good news is that there is hope for recovery from burnout. And there are warning signs that can be used to prevent you or those close to you from ever experiencing burnout.

That good news is our reason for writing this book.

DON HAWKINS

1
WHAT IS BURNOUT, AND WHO GETS IT?

No one expected Catherine to experience burnout, but that's exactly what happened. A slender, energetic blonde with sparkling brown eyes and a quick wit, Catherine was raised in east Texas, the third of four daughters, Catherine grew up in a balanced, caring home. She served as the president of her youth group in high school.

During her early years, however, another drive also began developing with her. As Catherine puts it, "My sisters did well, so I felt pressure to do well, to be smart like they were." Although personable and extremely attractive—she later worked as a model—Catherine had a poor self-concept. "I just didn't think very much of myself: I felt the need to prove myself all the time. Even though my parents were loving and accepting, I put a lot of pressure on myself to do well. For example, in school I expected to make straight A's even though I wasn't an A student."

Those internal pressures hit head-on with external stress in college and nursing school, where Catherine began to experience the warning signs of burnout. "There wasn't a lot of time for rest. After classes all day there was work in the hospital, and I often skipped meals and sometimes slept four or five hours a night." During that time, Catherine also started modeling to help pay bills. That added more pressure to her schedule. "There was no time for outside activities or hobbies, just for school and work."

Soon Catherine began having trouble sleeping. She says, "I just couldn't handle the pressure. I cried a lot; my grades began dropping; I just felt exhausted all the time. When I finally finished school, I didn't want to be a nurse or even be around doctors, nurses, or medicine. In fact, I didn't care if I ever took my state board exams. I graduated from nursing school a semester late, decided to forget about nursing, and went to work as a secretary. I was really burned out."

Burnout is when one's attitude becomes "a job is a job is a job," according to Edelwich and Brodsky, authors of one of the first books on the subject. To them, job burnout is when people get to the point of just putting in their time, avoiding making waves, and just barely getting by or going through the motions.[1]

Psychologist Herbert Feudenberger, who is generally credited with coining the term *burnout*, says that burnout is a depletion of energy and a feeling of being overwhelmed by others' problems.[2]

According to psychologist Christina Maslach, an early researcher of the problem, burnout is "a syndrome of emotional exhaustion, depersonalization, and reduced personal accomplishment that can occur among individuals who do 'people work' of some kind."[3]

In our own experience in counseling, burnout victims show those same three factors. Feeling physically and emotionally exhausted, victims frequently cannot face the future, and they detach themselves from interpersonal closeness. Sensing themselves to be drained emotionally, they also suffer spiritually.

The detachment leads to depersonalization—looking down on people, reacting negatively to them, and developing an attitude of "I wish people would go away and leave me alone."

That attitude, coupled with a feeling of emotional exhaustion—especially when seen in workers in the caring professions—results in a reduction in personal accomplishment. A feeling of diminishing accomplishment leads to stronger feelings of personal inadequacy, which further reduces accomplishment. And thus the vicious cycle of burnout is established.

Numerous mental health professionals and business consultants believe that burnout is a major reason American industry today has such a hard time achieving gains in productivity.[4]

FOUR SIGNS OF BURNOUT

Four significant words, *faint, weary, weak,* and *stumble,* are frequently given in descriptions of burnout. Each of them can apply to those suffering from burnout today.

FAINT

This term describes one who is about to pass out from a lack of nourishment. Most of us have experienced times when we have gone many hours without proper nourishment and perhaps without rest. Today's burnout victim, because of long hours, inability to sleep, and perhaps poor eating habits, tends perpetually to feel at the point of fainting.

WEARY

An individual suffering from burnout is characterized by perpetual exhaustion. Like a rubber band stretched beyond its capacity, he or she has lost elasticity. A college student drove himself during two rigorous semesters of work and study, climaxed by several all-night sessions of cramming in preparation for exams. After staying up all night before his most crucial exam, he fell asleep a half-hour before the exam was scheduled to begin. He slept through the exam, failed the course, and eventually dropped out of school. He suffered the consequences of his burnout.

Christina Maslach describes this aspect well:

> Burnout—the word evokes images of a final, flickering flame; of a charred and empty shell; of dying embers and cold, gray ashes. . . . Once fired up about their involvement with other people—excited, full of energy, dedicated, willing to give tremendously of themselves for others . . . [burnout victims] did give . . . and give and give, until finally there was nothing left to give any more. The teapot was empty, the battery was drained, the circuit was overloaded—they had burned out.[5]

WEAK

The burnout victim suffers a drop in his concentration level and in his ability to produce. Since we often tend to judge people on their ability to produce, there is often a parallel drop in feelings of self-worth. The decline in the ability to concentrate often results from, and enhances, anxiety. The anxious individual has become distracted, divided in his attention. As a result, he or she is unable to function at previous levels of efficiency.

The student who slept through his exam also illustrates a fourth significant characteristic that parallels that of today's burnout victims. The individual suffering from burnout is like an accident looking for a place to happen, to "stumble and fall." He is headed for a disaster—a blowup in a personal relationship, a physical collapse, or even a moral failure. That individual is likely to crash, unless his burnout is dealt with properly. Indeed, college students and other young people are among the most likely to suffer from burnout and its devastating characteristics as they start life on their own with all their might, but not knowing their own limitations.

THE ROLE OF STRESS

One of the most common definitions of burnout describes it as a loss of enthusiasm, energy, idealism, perspective, and purpose. It can be viewed as a state of mental, physical, and spiritual exhaustion brought on by continued stress.

Although a certain amount of stress is common, perhaps inevitable, and some stress is positive, too much stress over too long a time can result in burnout. Too much burnout, combined with too little application of coping techniques, can lead to clinical depression. We might view this on a continuum:

Stress $\longrightarrow$ Burnout $\longrightarrow$ Depression

Dr. Hans Selye, probably the most widely recognized authority on stress, defines stress as our body's response to any demand made upon it. He divides stress into two types: (1) *distress*—excessive levels of continued, damaging stress, and (2) *eustress*—a good, positive kind of stress one feels at times of happiness, fulfillment, or satisfaction.[6]

Although some stress is necessary for everyday living and, in lesser amounts, even for learning and growth, large, continued (chronic) amounts of stress, even *eustress,* can debilitate people. We do not want to eliminate all stress from our lives, but we do need to learn how to better handle and manage the necessary stresses of life.

BURNOUT OF THE WHOLE MAN

Too much stress and burnout affect the whole person—physically, emotionally, and spiritually. Physical symptoms can include anything from ulcers and digestive upsets to coronary problems. Often a burnout victim experiences a constant sense of fatigue, coupled with an inability to sleep. Emotionally, a burnout victim often suffers from depression. That results from being angry with oneself because of an inability to function at one's previous high performance level. Spiritually, burnout victims often reflect extreme anxiety over proving one's self-worth by serving others. In addition, they frequently feel life to be empty of real meaning or purpose.

Each of us is a potential target for burnout. Increasingly we find symptoms showing up in lawyers, physicians, housewives, psychologists, social workers, police officers, ministers, parents, computer professionals, nurses, industrial workers, secretaries, counselors, corporate executives, managers, teachers, and students. Half the parents in America, according to professor Joseph Procaccini, as well as one of five people in the helping professions today, according to an Alban Institute survey, suffer burnout.

One of the tragic paradoxes of burnout is that the people who tend to be the most dedicated, devoted, committed, responsible, highly motivated, educated, enthusiastic, promising, and energetic suffer from burnout. Why? Partially because those people are idealistic and perfectionistic. They expect too much of themselves as well as of others. Also, since they started out performing above average, others continue to expect those early, record-breaking results over the long haul, even though no one would expect a runner in the one-hundred-yard dash to keep up his speed in a cross-country run.

Burnout is:

- a parent who feels overly responsible when a child does something seriously wrong
- a nurse in a large hospital who takes her time or even ignores a patient's buzzer request for attention
- a mental health worker who doesn't seem to care anymore
- a factory worker who goes to lunch and doesn't return
- an alcohol rehabilitation counselor who drinks more and more, while complaining about his clients who drink
- a business executive who finds himself unable to function at his previous level
- a doctor who finds himself avoiding certain patients

- a salesman who has become so depressed that he is considering suicide
- a homemaker who finds herself in total despair after taking on too many activities
- a missionary who uses a relatively minor health problem as an excuse to escape the burdens and frustrations of living in a foreign culture
- an artist who senses that his creativity is expressionless
- a school principal griping about her teachers
- a teacher griping about her students

Those examples are taken from actual cases of burnout treated in our clinic. More about these individuals, their particular symptoms, and their recoveries will be given in later chapters.

BURNOUT IN HUMAN SERVICES

Job burnout is generally the end result of prolonged job-related or personal stress. The helping professions—nurses, doctors, pastors, social workers, and therapists, for example—seem to be particularly prone to burnout. Why? Human service workers, who deal with other people's personal problems, are employed in highly stressful occupations.

We've encountered a psychologist who left his profession to go to work in an oil field, a social worker who left her job to open up a ceramics shop, and a teacher who abandoned his field for a sales position. All of them had one thing in common: they were dedicated people in human service professions who left their careers not just because of salary considerations but because they were disillusioned and headed toward burnout unless they changed their outlook or their profession.

Many people change jobs because they are burned out. One man left his job as a psychologist to work in an oil field, another left a stable and secure administrative position in state government with a fixed salary to join the staff of a private psychiatric clinic. Even though his monthly salary would no longer be guaranteed, he preferred practicing individual and group therapy to doing reams of institutional bureaucratic paperwork, which was leaving him increasingly frustrated and burned out.

THE THREE BURNOUT AREAS

MENTAL

Burnout shows up mentally in the form of a feeling of disillusionment or failure as a person or worker. Signs of anger, cynicism, negativism, or increased irritability spring up. Burnout victims may feel frustrated by a sense of helplessness, hopelessness, or self-doubt, which then may lead to depression. Another common sign is guilt—false guilt over trying to be overly responsible or committed, a feeling of not doing something perfectly or well enough. Other symptoms of mental, or emotional, burnout include apathy, difficulty concentrating or paying attention, decreased self-esteem, feelings of disenchantment, disillusionment, disorientation, or confusion.

PHYSICAL

Throughout the years of our counseling, we have observed that continued stress and burnout may bring on backaches, neck aches, headaches, migraines, insomnia, loss of appetite (or a never-satisfied appetite), ulcers, high blood pressure, constant colds, digestive problems, allergies, or, in the most severe forms, heart attacks and strokes.

In many people, unrelieved, unresolved tension and stress result in their turning to alcohol or drugs, either prescription or over-the-counter, for temporary relief. The decreased energy and fatigue symptomatic of drugs tend to worsen an already burned-out feeling.

SPIRITUAL

Some people experience spiritual exhaustion with burnout. Such individuals seem to have lost perspective and have failed to recognize their own limits. They usually experience a gradually increasing feeling that God is powerless, and that they themselves are the only ones with the power to help in their current situation. Without realizing what they are doing, they refuse—consciously or unconsciously —to rely on God's power, and try to play God themselves. They may drop times of personal worship or spiritual meditation, only to feel as if they are in a spiritual vacuum where nothing or no one appears to be able to help. Then as time passes, they realize that their own power and energies are not enough either. They become disillusioned or feel like giving up, believing that others, including God, have given up on them.

RECOVERY

At the beginning of this chapter we learned of Catherine's experience with burnout, which parallels that of many people today. Some never recover, but Catherine did. In fact, the secretarial job she took was at our Minirth-Meier Clinic.

And how did Catherine recover from burnout? "I first recognized that I was burned out; then I began doing something about it. I learned to take care of myself physically. I cultivated my spiritual life. I developed outside interests. And perhaps most important of all, I learned not to be so hard on myself, to allow myself to fail occasionally, and to forgive myself when I did fail."

We will explore the symptoms of burnout—the warning signs— to help those who may be approaching burnout recognize the dangers before they become devastating. We will examine significant causes of burnout, including early life factors, personality factors, stress and environment factors, and a surprisingly significant element to which we all can be susceptible.

Finally, we will discuss positive steps for reversing burnout, steps that, if taken, can make it possible for former burnout victims such as Catherine to lead healthy, productive, balanced lives.

Burnout is serious, but for those who are feeling its effects, there is hope.

NOTES

1. Jerry Edelwich with Archie Brodsky, *Burn-Out: Stages of Disillusionment in the Helping Profession* (New York: Human Science, 1980).
2. Herbert Feudenberger and Geraldine Richelson, *Burn-Out* (New York: Anchor, Doubleday, 1980), p. 13.
3. Christian Maslach, *Burnout—The Cost of Caring* (Englewood Cliffs, N.J.: Prentice-Hall, 1982), p. 3.
4. For a survey of numerous research articles on the subject, see T. F. Riggar, *Stress Burnout: An Annotated Bibliography* (Carbondale, Ill.: Southern Illinois U., 1985).
5. Maslach, *Burnout*, p. 3.
6. Hans Selye, *The Stress of Life* (New York: McGraw-Hill, 1956; rev. 1976), p. 74.

2
WARNING:
DOWNWARD SPIRAL AHEAD

In the fall of 1900, a massive hurricane struck the Texas gulf coast. The city of Galveston, lying squarely in the path of the storm, bore the brunt of the hurricane winds and accompanying tidal wave. More than six thousand people lost their lives.

Today, more than eight decades later, when hurricanes roar across the Atlantic to hit the east or south coasts, only a few lives are lost. Why? Because advance warning techniques have improved vastly since the turn of the century. Now hurricane watches and warnings are widely broadcast. And people in threatened areas heed the storm warnings and evacuate to safety.

Just as meteorologists can now recognize certain signs as warnings of an approaching hurricane, so psychologists today can recognize storm warnings of another kind—symptoms of approaching burnout that need to be heeded. Such warnings tend to build on top of one another.

THE WORKAHOLIC—MOST LIKELY CANDIDATE

Although anyone can be subject to burnout, one personality type seems to be particularly prone to that condition. Most of the case examples listed in chapter 1 were "Type A" obsessive-compulsive* personalities. They are the kind of people who tend to be the most vulnerable to potential burnout. Often described as workaholics, they are marked by four characteristics: (1) a hectic schedule, (2) a strong achievement orientation, (3) an inability to say no, and

* See the glossary at the back of the book for definitions of this and other terms.

(4) a tendency toward frequent cardiac problems. Such workaholic personalities often show the following symptoms of potential burnout.

The major source of self-esteem and pleasure is work and productive activity. Obviously, some amount of pleasure and self-esteem should be received from work. However, since many people received only conditional love from their parents during childhood, when they were doing what pleased their parents, they condition themselves to feel significant only if they are being productive.

The major drive of obsessive-compulsive or workaholic individuals is a need to achieve control. That includes a need to control self, others, circumstances, and one's environment.

Burnout involves unfulfilled expectations, being worn down and tired out because what one thought would happen hasn't come about. Unfulfilled expectations relate basically to rewards that were expected but not received, such as happiness, praise, attention, a sense of satisfaction, or a sense of well-being or security.

Often, unfulfilled expectations occur because those expectations have been too high. If you lower your expectations to more realistic ones, you are less likely to burn out. (Of course, if you lower them to the point that you want to "just forget the whole thing," you are probably already in burnout!)

More than 90 percent of physicians and 75 percent of ministers who have been tested through the Minirth-Meier Clinic lean primarily toward obsessive-compulsive personality traits. Many of these may tend to "play God" over their staff, refusing to delegate control over even the least significant responsibility or problem.

THE SPIRITUAL ELEMENT

A lack of spiritual "daily bread" often compounds the burnout victim's self-efforts. Often, when one feels the pressure of burnout, the first thing to be eliminated is the time for personal reflection, meditation, and spiritual devotion. The pressures of a busy schedule, coupled with an increasing inability to keep up, crowd out a time for meditating on the Bible, which is essential to keeping a sharp edge spiritually, mentally, and physically. Rather than meditating on Scripture, burnout victims often spend time simply worrying about the problems that are pressing in on them.

SIGNS OF BURNOUT

EMOTIONAL EXHAUSTION

Herbert Freudenberger notes that lack of energy associated with feelings of tiredness and trouble keeping up with one's usual round of activities are the first warning signs of burnout.[1]

Emotional exhaustion differs from the pleasant physical exhaustion that comes after a good workout. Two case histories illustrate this contrast. Tim and Marty are both business executives in their forties. Tim rises early every day, eats a good breakfast, works hard for eight hours, plays handball in the afternoon following his work three days a week. It's good aerobic exercise. As a result, he feels exhausted, but as he puts it, "It's a good exhaustion." Tim has stirred up the endorphins in his brain, attaining the aerobic exercise Dr. Ken Cooper and others say is so essential for a healthy physical well-being.

Marty, on the other hand, seldom exercises, usually considering himself too busy getting things done for the company. Marty is currently trying to balance five projects, struggling in his relationships with people, and is frequently angry for no apparent reason. He arose from bed one Saturday with an entire day off before him, but he felt so emotionally drained that he couldn't tackle a single one of the twelve projects he had listed to consider working on for that day. Unrealistically he had hoped to complete at least half of them. Marty was emotionally exhausted.

DETACHMENT

The next warning sign, according to Freudenberger, is putting distance between ourselves and other people, particularly those people with whom we have had close relationships. People on the edge of burnout have less and less time and energy for relationships, since more and more of their time and efforts are concentrated on just "keeping up." Continuing the two case histories above, Tim enjoys people and doesn't mind interruptions, although occasionally he closes his door to concentrate on an important project at hand. He prides himself on having an "open door" policy. He doesn't even mind when his oldest daughter drops in with his brand new grandbaby. Marty, on the other hand, has become extremely irritable with people, greatly bothered by interruptions. Most of the staff in the office have learned that whether Marty's door is open or not, it's best to treat it as closed. Sometimes he lashes out verbally with sarcastic barbs; at other times he simply withdraws, his only communication a hoarse grunt. Marty finds it difficult to name one person in his life he enjoys being with. He is plagued by "depersonalization," a desire to withdraw from people.

REDUCED ACCOMPLISHMENT

This is, in effect, working harder and harder but accomplishing less and less. It's the same phenomenon that occurs when a car gets stuck in a snowbank. The inexperienced driver revs up the engine, spins the wheels. The harder the wheels spin, the more heat and friction are generated, the less effective are the efforts to dislodge the car from the snowbank. Although at times Tim feels frustrated because of the overload of pressures and responsibilities, generally speaking he feels pretty good about himself and about what he's doing. Some things he does extremely well, other things, not as well. But he cuts himself enough slack to recognize that, and he can feel good about limited accomplishments.

Marty, on the other hand, simply drives himself harder and harder when he realizes that he's exhausted or not as efficient. Consequently, he spends a great deal of time sitting at his desk, staring into the middle distance or at an incomprehensible spreadsheet, or at other times, hunched over his computer terminal, three lines thumped into the word processor and a monumental block between Marty and the rest of the overdue report. Tim is coping relatively well with the stresses of life. Marty is burned out.

In addition to these three major sysmptoms of burnout, there may be others, including:

BOREDOM AND CYNICISM

Freudenberger states that boredom and cynicism are "natural companions. One begets the other; detachment begets them both." The burnout victim "begins to question the value of friendships and activities—even of life itself."[2]

INCREASED IMPATIENCE AND IRRITABILITY

Usually burnout victims are people who have been able to do things quickly. However, as burnout takes hold, their ability to accomplish things diminishes, and their impatience grows, leading to flare-ups with others. They often blame family and co-workers for things that are their own fault.

A SENSE OF OMNIPOTENCE

Some burnout victims may have persistent thoughts such as, *Nobody can do my job better than I,* or, *Only I can do it, nobody else.* They may also think subconsciously—while denying it consciously —that *I'm more powerful and see things more correctly than anyone else.* Obviously, that form of exaggerated subconscious thinking, which is not unusual among burnout victims, borders on the delusional.

FEELINGS OF BEING UNAPPRECIATED

Another warning sign Freudenberger has identified is frustration because others do not express appreciation.[3] Burnout victims experience complex feelings of bitterness, anger, and resentment because they are not being appreciated for their efforts. Why not? Because those added efforts that they put forth, instead of producing added results, are generating reduced results. Rather than acknowledging that, they blame others for not appreciating them.

CHANGE OF WORK STYLE

Reduced results, conflicts with colleagues, and other work-related contacts will eventually cause one of two things to happen. Either the victim will withdraw from decisive leadership and work habits, or he or she will seek to compensate for the conflicts by becoming more and more tyrannical, demanding, or inflexible. This response only causes the cycle of burnout to worsen.

PARANOIA

Once burnout has taken long-term hold, it is but a small step from feeling unappreciated to feeling mistreated or threatened. The advanced burnout victim may sense that someone is "out to get me."

DISORIENTATION

As burnout continues long-term, the victim will have increasing difficulty with wandering thought processes. Speech patterns will falter. Concentration spans will become increasingly limited, and the ability to remember names, dates, or even what he or she started to say will diminish. The victim may jokingly refer to having a problem of increasing old age or senility, but the real problem is increasing agitation and inward stress.

PSYCHOSOMATIC COMPLAINTS

Physical ailments seem more conventional and therefore easier to accept than emotional ailments. The following physical complaints tend to flourish in burnout victims: headaches, lingering colds, backaches, and similar complaints. Those physical symptoms are frequently induced or at least prolonged by the burnout victim's emotional stress. The complaints may have real physical causes, but, more than likely, they are brought on by emotional stress, which the sufferer may not want to admit. Often, the victim focuses more on physical complaints than usual, as those become the scapegoat, on one end of the spectrum, for the person's emotional condition and, on the other end, for the negative work results of his burnout.

DEPRESSION

There are differences between a generally depressed state and the form of depression that usually signifies burnout. In burnout, "the depression is usually temporary, specific, and localized, pertaining more or less to one area of life."[4] The depression of most burnout victims is apt to be anger at other people for causing his or her problems.

MAJOR DEPRESSION

Some depressed burnout victims will experience major depression, a *generally* depressed state that is usually prolonged and pervades all areas of a person's life. Furthermore, the generally depressed person has turned blame for negative circumstances toward self. Instead of being angry with others, he or she tends to feel guilty for everything that is going wrong.

SUICIDAL THINKING

As depression associated with burnout progresses, the result can be suicidal thinking. Suicide is the tenth leading cause of death in the U.S. Ten percent of individuals who make suicidal gestures eventually die of suicide. Certain personality types, such as the hysterical personality, may make suicide threats or gestures that are manipulative in nature only. However, obsessive-compulsive personalities are more likely to make actual suicide attempts.

In the next chapter we will take a closer look at ten burnout victims and consider the question, Are *you* a candidate for burnout?

NOTES

1. Herbert Freudenberger and Geraldine Richelson, *Burn-Out* (New York: Anchor, Doubleday, 1980), p. 62.
2. Ibid., p. 63.
3. Ibid., p. 64.
4. Ibid., p. 66.

3
ARE YOU A
CANDIDATE FOR BURNOUT?

The lives of the burnout victims mentioned in chapter 1 represent the burnout syndrome in action. Let's take another look at their stories. As you read, compare their experience with yours.

TEN VICTIMS OF BURNOUT

- *The parent who felt overly responsible when a child did something seriously wrong*

A mother, Ellen, did a reasonably good job in raising her children, as did her husband. Yet one child grew up to live in almost total rebellion. When Ellen looked back on her career as a mother, she remembered circumstances in which she didn't act in the way she believed a perfect mother should have. As a result, she blamed herself totally for the child's failure. She suffered from false guilt, which led to major depression.

- *The nurse in a large hospital who took her time or even ig-nored patients' buzzer requests for attention*

A conscientious nurse, Anne normally took good care of her patients. Yet, because of her long working hours, plus grudges she held toward her supervisor, Anne became clinically depressed. Her supervisor expected too much, such as requiring her to work over-time on many weekends. Afraid of losing her job, Anne never com-plained about the long hours. Finally, she reached the point of losing her motivation, which resulted in poor work. When she got to the point of ignoring patients' buzzers, Anne finally sought our counseling help.

Anne's symptoms included exhaustion, detachment (from patients), cynicism, feelings of being unappreciated, a change of work style, paranoia (fear of being fired if she requested fewer hours), and depression (accompanied by anger toward her supervisor for her problems).

- *The mental health worker who didn't seem to care anymore*

Jeanne carried a heavy load of counseling in a psychiatric treatment unit. She helped many individuals who suffered from depression, and she loved her patients. Yet talking to people fifty to sixty hours a week about depression finally got to Jeanne. She began to get clinically depressed herself. Jeanne's symptoms included exhaustion, boredom and cynicism, feelings of being unappreciated, and depression.

- *The factory worker who went to lunch and didn't return*

An eighteen-year-old recent high school graduate, Dan had landed a factory job that paid well. At first he liked the job. The work wasn't difficult, he had opportunity to meet people of all ages, and "it sure beat doing school assignements." But spending all of his time on an assembly line, tightening screws, and repeating the process thousands of times a day, all day long, forty hours a week, eventually began to get to him. Because of the monotony, the noise level, and the heat in the nonair-conditioned factory building, Dan became burned out. One day he went to lunch and didn't come back, having decided to quit his job.

Dan's symptoms included exhaustion, boredom, feelings of being unappreciated, irritability, and depression (accompanied by anger toward those who were making him work in an undesirable and unpleasant work environment).

- *The alcohol-rehabilitation counselor who was drinking more and more, while complaining about his clients who drank*

For most of his life, Lewis had not been a drinker. He liked people and enjoyed working with them, but he was finding himself becoming more and more frustrated. A number of the alcoholics with whom he was working were poorly motivated and were not getting better. They simply would not do what they needed to do to overcome their addiction. This made Lewis angry because he wanted them to get better, both because he loved them and also because their refusal to get better made him feel powerless.

As a result, Lewis became increasingly angry and ultimately began drinking himself. The drinking led to greater depression than before because alcohol tended to lower the serotonin level in his brain. Lewis began drinking to excess, which temporarily numbed his pain. However, the day following a drinking bout he would feel even more depressed.

Lewis's symptoms included detachment, impatience and irritability, feelings of being unappreciated, and major depression (from both physical and psychological causes).

- *The business executive who found himself unable to function at his previous level*

A highly energetic and intelligent man, George had risen to the presidency of his company by the time he was forty. When he reached fifty, however, he was still trying to maintain the sixty-hour week that had helped carry him to the top of his company, plus sustain a multitude of civic and other activities as well. When he found he could no longer do all that, George began to get angry—angry at himself for getting older, angry at his Creator for allowing him to get older, angry at the aging process itself and angry because he was no longer able to concentrate or perform as well. This anger brought on depression, which caused his concentration level to become even worse.

George's symptoms included exhaustion, impatience and irritability, change of work style, disorientation (involving the lowered concentration level), and depression (related to his anger).

- *The salesman whose depression led to suicidal thinking*

A middle-aged man with some health problems, Bill occasionally had experienced bouts with depression over the years. After turning forty, he suffered two significant losses: he was terminated from his job, and his marriage was in the process of breaking up. As a result, he had to work longer hours for less money at a job that gave him little satisfaction. His marital conflict aggravated his job-related burnout and left him with no emotional support. Bill's strong personal need to achieve, coupled with the hopelessness he felt concerning his circumstances, led to depression and suicidal thinking.

Bill's symptoms included exhaustion, detachment (from former colleagues, as well as from his wife), boredom (in an unchallenging job), feelings of being unappreciated, psychosomatic complaints, major depression (involving hopelessness and guilt for all his problems), and suicidal thinking.

- *The missionary who used a relatively minor health problem as an excuse to escape the burdens and frustrations of living in a foreign culture*

After several years of service as foreign missionary, Jack found that he really did not enjoy missionary work as much as he thought he would and became convinced he had made a mistake. He thought he could serve better in North America in a different capacity. Yet he was embarrassed to come back and tell his supporters that he had decided not to be a missionary any longer. Instead Jack blamed a relatively minor health problem on his decision to return. Then he felt guilty for using that as an excuse.

Jack's burnout symptoms included exhaustion from "culture shock" (which normally involves impatience and irritability when encountering many obstacles in a different or slower culture that make it impossible to accomplish as much as we can in our own culture), withdrawal from decisive leadership, psychosomatic complaints (which had some basis, though relatively minor), and depression involving guilt—guilt from giving up on his missionary calling, and guilt from blaming his withdrawal on what was at best a half-truth.

- *The homemaker who found herself in total despair after taking on too many activities*

A workaholic homemaker, Lisa had been the oldest daughter in her family. Her mother had been critical of her while she was growing up; no matter what she did it wasn't quite enough. Her school grades were usually A's with a few B's. Whenever she got a B, her mother criticized her.

When Lisa married, she carried her workaholism and obsessive-compulsive desire to please into her marriage and motherhood experience. She did a great deal for her children, including home schooling them. Lisa thought for them, controlled them, and taught them herself, even though she lived in an area that had good public schools.

Lisa was active in a number of organizations, taught Sunday school, was president of the women's society, served as church organist, and sang special solos and duets. She was a workaholic career woman, even though hers wasn't a paid career. As a result of her workaholism and striving to live up to her own mother's expectations of having a "perfect" daughter, Lisa suffered a major depression and burnout.

Lisa's symptoms included exhaustion, impatience and irritability, feelings of being unappreciated, change of work style, paranoia, disorientation, and major depression (accompanied by guilt from not doing everything perfectly).

All of these people, after a time spent under the care of our clinic, were able to reverse their burnout spiral and recover. Much of the information that helped them do that is explained in this book. Had this book been accessible to them, some of them would have had the information they needed to overcome their burnout without direct professional care. Others would have been helped by this information but would still have needed special care before their burnout spiral could have been reversed.

MEASURING BURNOUT

How can you tell if *you* are burning out?

Burnout is approaching:

- if you find yourself griping more and more and enjoying life less and less
- if you can't stand people
- if you want to withdraw
- if you feel like the school bus driver who said, "I love my bus; I like my route, but I hate every single student who rides my bus"

- if you have trouble separating people from their performance, especially if no one's performance matches up to your rigorous standards
- if you are experiencing drug or alcohol abuse
- if you have had a major blowup—yelling at people or collapsing in tears
- if you have felt "paralyzed" when you needed to take action

Burnout is probably acute:

- if you have experienced a coronary or other serious physical problem
- if you are experiencing an emotional breakdown or suicidal feelings
- if you are involved in "acting-out" behavior—an affair, an arrest for driving while intoxicated (burnout doesn't excuse our behavior but may explain why it occurs)
- if you are completely overcome by exhaustion or uncontrollable anger

Burnout has become chronic:

- if you continually find yourself withdrawing physically from your job
- if you have trouble maintaining contact with people—even eye contact or verbal communication
- if you quit your job without good reason
- if you lack the emotional energy to handle the daily hassles of family life
- if you refuse to discuss your problems or acknowledge a need for help

Where are you on the burnout scale? Is burnout approaching? Is it acute? Are you clinically burned out? How many of the above statements are true of you?

BURNOUT INVENTORY

The time for taking action to break the downward spiral of burnout is at the first recognition of any storm warnings. Burnout is a reversible spiral. The key is to begin action immediately to take care of oneself and to reverse the burnout.

If you believe you are headed for burnout, here is a way to further test yourself for symptoms. Check those statements with which you agree.

1. More and more, I find that I can hardly wait for quitting time to come so that I can leave work.
2. I feel as if I'm not doing any good at work these days.
3. I am more irritable than I used to be.
4. I'm thinking about changing jobs.
5. Lately I've become more cynical and negative.
6. I have more headaches (or backaches or other physical symptoms) than usual.
7. Often I feel hopeless, like saying, "Who cares?"
8. I drink more now or take tranquilizers just to cope with everyday stress.
9. My energy level is not what it used to be. I'm tired all the time.
10. I feel a lot of pressure and responsibility at work these days.
11. My memory is not as good as it used to be.
12. I don't seem to concentrate or pay attention as well as I have in the past.
13. I don't sleep as well as I used to.
14. My appetite is decreased these days (or, I can't seem to stop eating).
15. I feel unfulfilled and disillusioned.
16. I'm not as enthusiastic about work as I was a year or two ago.
17. I feel like a failure at work. All the work I've done hasn't been worth it.
18. I can't seem to make decisions as easily as I once did.
19. I find I'm doing fewer things at work that I like or do well.
20. I often ask myself, *Why bother? It doesn't really matter anyhow.*
21. I don't feel adequately rewarded or noticed for all the work I've done.
22. I feel helpless, as if I can't see any way out of my problems.

23. People have told me I'm too idealistic about my job.
24. I think my career has come to a dead end.

Count up your check marks. If you agree with a majority of those statements, then you may be feeling burnout and be in need of professional help or at least a change in lifestyle.

4
THE ROOT
CALLED BITTERNESS

In our psychiatric clinic, two women, Lucy and Linda, were treated for suicidal depression. Both of them came from similar backgrounds. Although they grew up in different parts of the country, both were oldest daughters. Both had strong musical talents at an early age and continued to use those gifts after they were grown. Both were also involved in teaching.

Yet as adults both became severely depressed to the point of being unable to function. Lucy, in fact, had developed multiple personalities. Both women came to our clinic as the result of strong suicidal thoughts.

After months and years of treatment, each began making significant progress. Lucy ultimately became healthy and functional. Linda, however, continued to struggle.

In examining the similarities and differences between these two women, one key factor became evident. Both women had been sexually and emotionally abused by their fathers and by other male family members at an early age. For years, both had blocked out that repeated abuse from their conscious minds. When compassionate counselors helped them to remove the blocks that had led to their severe depression, consciousness of what had happened to them came to the surface.

When they became aware of what had happened, however, their responses were somewhat different. Over a period of time, Lucy, though appropriately angry over her abuse, chose to forgive her father and others for what had happened. Linda, on the other hand, retained a measure of bitterness and resentment. She continued to harbor feelings of anger and animosity and could think or talk of little else. As a result, her process of healing and restoration was severely hampered.

Both Lucy and Linda had experienced severe burnout as wives and mothers. However, one was able to recover and experience restoration. The other did not experience the same measure of recovery. Why? Because of the relationship between bitterness and burnout. In our counseling, we have seen literally hundreds of examples that verify a close connection between bitterness and resentment and the symptoms that we call burnout.

Some time ago, a woman came for counseling about the pressures under which her husband labored. During the course of her initial conversation, she observed, "I really don't have any problems myself." However, she expressed complaints about several people, a number of her office colleagues, and even some incidents that had occurred in her family years before. During the counseling session, she asserted that both she and her husband were burned out. It took some time to demonstrate to her the connection between her feelings of burnout and her bitterness toward the people about whom she had complained.

THE CAUSES OF BITTERNESS

WRONG MOTIVES OF JEALOUSY

We frequently see bitterness associated with jealousy. Examples include successful attorneys and other professionals who envy the abilities of their colleagues, college students consumed with jealousy toward fellow students whom they perceive as having more insight into their studies, and business leaders who are envious of others who have seen more outward evidences of success in their careers.

CONDITIONAL LOVE

We have heard wives assert, "Nothing I do ever pleases him. I can't cook, can't keep house, can't take care of the children, or can't balance the checkbook to please him." Sometimes we hear husbands in marital counseling making the same assertions. One husband even used such assertions to justify his having an affair with another woman. His rationale? "I'm not sure I love her anymore."

We believe such bitterness and petty criticism often results from an underlying lack of unconditional love. All of us have, at times, been guilty of practicing conditional love, which is based on the performance of the one we supposedly love. Conditional love produces harshness and bitterness in both husbands and wives. Frequently this leads to marital burnout. However, both conditional love and marital burnout can be reversed.

WRONG RESPONSE TO ADVERSITY

All of us at times suffer adverse circumstances. Sometimes these are the consequence of our failure, sometimes not. But, in reponse, if we fail to diligently pursue peace with all men and with God, bitterness may take root. As that bitterness grows and develops, often beneath the surface of our conscious thoughts, it becomes more and more a part of our outlook on life. The results are devastating, both to us and to those around us.

We are much better off, even in extreme adversity, when we choose to put aside or get rid of all bitterness and associated anger, outbursts of temper, ill will, or unkind words. Bitterness may grow and develop for years, simply because we nourish it by talking about offenses that have occurred. We voice our hurts to anyone who will listen and even to those who would rather not. In quiet moments, rather than reflecting on life's positives, we spend our time focused on those hurtful moments.

THE SYMPTOMS OF BITTERNESS

One of the major lessons we learn from the field of medicine is that fever indicates the presence of an infection. Similarly, it has been our observation that murmuring, grumbling, griping, or complaining are related to bitterness. Griping, or "murmuring," as it has been called, is a common phenomenon and is present in the lives of many of us. It can show the underlying presence of bitterness.

GRIPING

To gripe or complain against circumstances, an authority figure, a parent, or an employer is a strong indicator of underlying bitterness either toward the authority figure or even against an authority from earlier in life. For example, frequent conflicts with an employer may indicate previous conflicts with a parent.

Joe bounced from job to job. He never seemed to be able to get along with any of his employers. And to hear Joe tell it, it was always their fault. He tried sales, management, customer service—a variety of positions. In each one he was recognized for his conscientious approach to his work. But ultimately he would lose his job due to conflicts with his employers.

Eventually Joe sought counseling. The end result was that he came to grips with long-buried conflicts with his father. Joe's persistent griping about his job circumstances and the treatment he received from his bosses were clear evidence of the presence of bitterness in his life.

INTERPERSONAL CONFLICT

A closely related symptom of bitterness is manifested in interpersonal conflicts. George was the classic yuppie. He graduated near the head of his class in business administration, moved into an important position in the family company, married his childhood sweetheart, and had two children. But George had trouble getting along with people. Even though his position at the company seemed secure—after all, his dad had founded it, and his brother was CEO— George eventually found himself forced to leave. When they learned he was leaving, George's fellow employees threw a party to celebrate—and didn't invite George. Everyone, it seemed, had some war story to tell about conflict with the man most employees had assumed would take over the company.

George experienced conflicts in other areas of his life as well. He was constantly carping at his neighbors over some alleged problem. Such intensity, even abusiveness, eventually led to the decline of his marriage. George had become conscientious about his personal faith. Nonetheless, he became involved in three different churches over a five-year span. From his perspective, none of them measured up to what he was looking for. But others saw it quite differently.

One church staff member put it this way: "George seemed to have a chip on his shoulder. Nothing anyone did was quite up to his exacting standards. He just seemed like a square peg in a round hole."

Eventually George's underlying personal bitterness over several very painful events in his life were recognized to be at the heart of his conflict.

INTENSE EMOTIONS

Intense emotions constitute a third symptom of hidden bitterness. Some people have strong surface emotions, whereas others demonstrate a more even temperament. In addition, some disorders, such as bipolar depression—or manic depressive disorder as it is commonly called—lead to ups and downs. We have found that the individual who exhibits a roller-coasterlike emotional ride through life frequently does so because of unresolved bitterness.

As a college student, Julia had been recognized as possessing great mental and academic ability. Her high school graduating class voted her most likely to succeed. But Julia struggled with college. One minute she was absolutely thrilled at the least little thing—a friendly greeting from an upperclassman she hoped to date, an A on a quiz in one of her classes. The next minute she was devastated, wiped out by a perceived slight from one of her roommates, completely dismayed by not being asked out by the same young man who had seemed so friendly between classes. Her emotional ups and downs finally drove Julia to the guidance counselor's office—somewhat to the relief of her roommates.

After several sessions, Julia finally acknowledged a layer of bitterness toward a young man with whom she had had a close relationship during high school—a relationship that had broken off in acrimonious fashion. However, it wasn't until years later in therapy that Julia was finally able to get to the bottom of her bitterness— emotional and sexual abuse at the hand of an uncle, which had occurred on several occasions during her early life. Julia's anger, even rage, over the abuse, was most understandable. But it had been buried, then prolonged into bitterness, which led to a storm of emotional instability.

UNREALISTIC EXPECTATIONS

Another crucial symptom of bitterness is something we call "undue expectations." Everyone has expectations. But most of us aren't aware of them. Sometimes it might be enlightening for us to play back tapes of some of our conversations with others—or even tapes of the thoughts that so frequently and clearly reveal what we expect. So often the internal conditioning we received in childhood causes us to expect far more of ourselves than we are capable of delivering.

Yet those of us who are hardest on ourselves usually find ourselves quite hard on others as well. We expect kind, understanding responses from wives who have been pushed to the brink by irritated children and malfunctioning appliances all day. We anticipate empathy and compassionate conversation from a husband who has spent the day wrestling with demands from an overzealous boss, plus an array of complaints from those who work in the department he manages. We expect mature understanding from a sixteen year old whose hormones and maturity level—or lack thereof—combine to bring about anything but a mature response to our parental demands.

Frequently we expect to be protected from cancer, traffic accidents, layoffs due to corporate takeovers and mergers, drops in income, automotive breakdowns, appliance breakdowns, or a score of other big or little causes of stress that may invade our lives.

INABILITY TO TRUST

Another symptom of underlying bitterness is a perfectionistic inability to trust. The individual who tends to become paranoid about trusting people or circumstances has frequently been deeply hurt in the past—and the effects of that pain in the form of bitterness continues to linger.

Charlotte called our radio talk show to say, "I'm constantly worried that something bad will happen to one of my two children. Whenever my husband is gone, I make them come down and sleep with me. Do you think that's unhealthy?" When we asked how old they were, she admitted they were eleven and nine. As we gently probed with questions, we discovered Charlotte had lost a baby to crib death, or sudden infant death syndrome. Finally she was able to pinpoint her problem, "I guess I really can't trust God. He let my baby die."

Fear has a specific object—for example, we fear cancer or AIDS, the consequence of a speeding ticket, or a trip to the dentist. On the other hand, anxiety's object is not specific. Yet both grow directly out of an inability to trust. The worry-prone, fearful personality has great difficulty trusting people or circumstances. Frequently anxious or fearful people say, "It's not really paranoia, it's insight." To which we reply, "Perhaps it's both." But one thing is sure, insight into these underlying emotions—especially bitterness over the pain we've been dealt by previous circumstances—can go a long way toward alleviating the kind of anxiety or fear that may contribute to burnout.

DENIAL

Some people practice a symptom of underlying bitterness that we have identified as denial. Many men and women are like Ralph—successful, well-dressed, purposeful—yet his face darkened with anger as he stated, "I'm not bitter, so don't start talking to me about anger." Then he quickly proceeded to disprove his claim. He had trouble remembering responsibilities in his work. His burnout had caused him to experience a great deal of confusion and reduced accomplishment on the job.

But Ralph could remember in clear detail the events—even individual incidents of conflict—that led to his self-described "messy divorce from that woman I was married to." Despite his protestations that, "I'm not bitter—I have forgiven her, even though she doesn't deserve it," bitterness leaked from every sentence he spoke.

LACK OF GRATITUDE

Another clear-cut symptom of bitterness is an absence of gratitude. Although a lack of gratitude seems to be a characteristic of the day in which we are living, frequent ungratefulness indicates bitterness. You see, bitterness is like cholesterol. It slows, then eventually blocks the life-stimulating flow of gratitude.

Judd was an angry eighteen year old. To hear him tell it, his parents were the two most unreasonable, uncaring, unfeeling people who had ever raised a son. They didn't care about him—they were only interested in themselves. They expected too much of him; even though they provided him with many nice things and were patient and loving, he didn't see it that way.

It wasn't until after a great deal of digging and probing that we discovered Judd was holding a grudge against his dad's career change when Judd was nine years old—a change that had caused the family to move across the country, separating Judd from two of his closest friends. Judd wasn't even aware of it—but he had a great deal of unresolved bitterness about that event from years past. Bitterness showed itself as ungratefulness.

A CALLOUSED APPROACH TO LIFE

Bitterness often manifests itself as an indifference or calloused approach to life—something we refer to at times as a "hard edge." Some people become calloused and insensitive to the feelings of others, or even to their own need for relationships with God and with people. Such a hardened emotional state is often difficult to reverse.

Rod was an electrician. He had spent much of his life working with pliers, electrical wiring, and similar tools. As a result, his hands were extremely calloused. On the surface, Rod seemed to be an easygoing, jovial sort of fellow—except when it came to spiritual and emotional issues. His ridicule of his wife's personal faith, and his gallows humor toward individuals in his family and office who suffered personal tragedy—all demonstrated that something emotionally was amiss.

Finally, after his marriage almost broke up and he nearly lost his job because of burnout, Rod's bitterness came to the surface. It seemed that Rod was still carrying a grudge over the death of his mother many years before. When he graduated from high school he had planned to go to college, but his mother became sick. She entered the hospital for surgery—the surgery was unsuccessful and left her in a nearly vegetative state. From Rod's perspective, it all happened because "the doctors botched the operation."

As a result, the family finances were drained, and money Rod's parents had set aside for him to attend college wound up being used tp pay medical bills. Rod entered the electrical union to which his dad belonged and ultimately became a second generation master electrician. But his bitterness toward the doctors who were unable to save his mother's life—and even toward his mother for dying and abandoning him—contributed significantly to both his marriage conflict and his job burnout.

In the next chapter we will further examine how bitterness leads to burnout.

5
MANIFESTATIONS
OF BITTERNESS

A flyer posted above the coffee pot in a downtown office spurred repeated outbursts of laughter. It featured a picture of a loaded barge, sailing under the New York City skyline. The inscription below the picture read, "Fabulous vacation opportunity at an incredibly reasonable price. Spend several months cruising scenic East Coast and Caribbean ports. Bask in warm sunshine. Enjoy getting away from the pressure of life. The price is extremely reasonable—if you can stand the smell."

The irony was that the barge was the infamous New York City garbage barge. Even more ironic, many of the people who laughed the loudest at the idea of taking a cruise with such a rank collection of refuse find themselves going through life carrying their own personal load of emotional garbage in the form of bitterness.

In fact, when a person feels tension from the past, the primary emotion is generally bitterness. Unresolved bitterness can turn any individual into a pitiful wreck while making those around him miserable as well. Bitterness is like the roots of poison ivy. It doesn't take a lot of the plant to cause a great deal of grief for the individual, the family, fellow workers, even those with whom we worship or enjoy recreational acitivies.

Some time ago a woman who chose to call herself Alice called our nationwide call-in talk show. She indicated that she had ruined her marriage by becoming involved in two extramarital affairs. She was currently working in a massage parlor. Her life was in shambles. When asked why, she pinpointed the problem quickly, "I really have strong feelings of bitterness against my husband—plus, I'm bitter toward my father for the abuses I suffered in childhood."

Although it's understandable for individuals to be angry—even to the point of rage—over physical, emotional, or sexual abuse, to harbor such anger in the form of bitterness is, to use the terminology of one mental health authority, "self-cannibalization." Research for our initial writing in this area showed that bitterness—even more than personal stress, workaholism, or Type A personality traits—is the primary cause of burnout.

Following a businessmen's conference, one man admitted, "I've been feeling burned out for some time. I always thought it was in connection with serving others. I never thought part of my burnout resulted from being bitter or resentful toward the demands placed on me, or toward several colleagues who attempted to have me fired many years ago."

A successful executive, with tears in his eyes, came up to one of the authors following a session on bitterness and burnout. "I've always considered myself to be a hard-driving Type A personality. I came to this conference feeling burned out. I was convinced it was because I was under a great deal of stress—and probably because I was a workaholic. In fact, I was proud of my workaholism. Tonight I came to grips for the first time with the fact that I've been bitter toward my dad for many years. He was extremely harsh, constantly criticizing us, never expressing love. He abused my mother, as well as the rest of us—and I've never forgiven him. I've always held a grudge against him, even looked for opportunities to get even. I can't believe how those feelings have poisoned my life. I'm sure now that's why I'm so drained, so burned out."

THREE COMPONENTS OF BITTERNESS

What is the nature of this root problem of bitterness that lies at the heart of so many of our emotional conflicts? We generally identify three components of bitterness. The first and most obvious is anger. The second is an element of time—in other words, anger is prolonged. The third is the motive—either conscious or subconscious —to get revenge. Let's consider these three components.

ANGER

Many people consider anger to be inherently bad, always wrong. In the past, some counselors have stated, "Never become angry. You shouldn't ever be angry. It's important always to be loving and forgiving." Anger is not inherently wrong. Anger is like the red light at an intersection. It is a signal—a signal to stop and consider what's going on; a warning of danger.

Becoming inappropriately angry, maintaining anger, or allowing anger to dominate our lives is wrong, just as running a red light is an offense for which we may receive a ticket—or worse, suffer the natural consequence of becoming involved in a traffic mishap. There will be times when we become angry. It's important for us to get in touch with our anger, understand what we are angry about and why, consider carefully the extent to which we should feel angry, then decide what to do about it.

Anger, basically, is an emotional response to a threat or a perceived threat to ourselves, our possessions, or our values. It is a basic emotion and frequently masks other hidden emotions such as fear. The physiological component of anger involves the triggering of the "fight or flight" mechanism, the pumping of adrenaline, constricting of the blood vessels, the quickening of the pulse, and those other physiologic components with which we are so familiar. In an earlier era, when men lived on the frontier and were subject to hostile attacks from Indians—who themselves were responding to the invasion of their lands by those who were not Native Americans—or to plundering outlaws of various backgrounds, the fight or flight mechanism could come in handy. It might mean the difference between life or death. Similarly, when an 86-pound, 5-foot woman was accosted in a shopping mall of a major city by two shoplifters, anger enabled her to attack one with a roundhouse right, grab her purse back from the other one, and outrun him to the nearest security post. Anger, though not always wrong, is a necessary component for bitterness.

THE TIME FACTOR

However, anger does not always lead to bitterness unless the second component is present. That ingredient is the prolonging of the emotion. The ancient Hebrews had a great idea—the time limit that should be placed on anger was sundown. In other words, anger should not last beyond the time at which the day's activities cease and people in that society went to bed. From our counseling practice, we know that the same principle is equally effective today. It is important to resolve whatever angry feelings we have prior to bedtime, not carrying them over to be ruminated on and perhaps even acted out.

Our colleague Dr. Les Carter, in his book *Putting the Past Behind,* defines bitterness as "profound grief accompanied by suppressed hostility toward seemingly unbearable circumstances."[1] Thus the anger is often prolonged long after its actual cause has disappeared. Resultant feelings of grief and hostility have much the same emotional effect as battery acid or other physically bitter substances.

Repressed anger needs to be appropriately and properly expressed. If we are angry with our mate, with our neighbor, or with a colleague at work, we need to confront those persons, if at all possible, and carefully and lovingly express our feelings before the day is over. To do otherwise is unhealthy spiritually, mentally, or physically.

Unfortunately, many of us are not very good at processing anger. For some of us, the most common method of processing anger is "aggressively"—shouting, giving criticism, griping. For others, a passive-aggressive approach may be preferred—giving the silent treatment, sulking, being lazy, or sabotaging.

In either case, when anger goes unresolved, it takes root, gradually sprouting into bitterness—that unsavory emotion which, like a cancer, spreads throughout the personality, producing devastating physical, emotional, and spiritual consequences.

REVENGE

The third basic component of anger is the conscious or subconscious motive to get even. The Hebrews in ancient times also had a practical and excellent law that basically required each individual to confront his neighbor over wrong and forgive, leaving vengeance up to God. How frequently have people said, "I'll get even. Vengeance is mine. I will repay . . . " Even though the individual making those statements may, when confronted, say, "I have no serious intention of getting revenge," there may be self-deception present—a denial of the true subconscious desire to get revenge.

There are numerous circumstances in which this revenge motive may push us in this direction. For example, as a child Lucinda repeatedly received condescending messages from the aunt with whom she came to live after her parents were killed in a traffic accident. She never allowed Lucinda to express any dissenting thoughts or feelings. For years Lucinda repressed her anger. Growing up in the late sixties, she became a part of the movement of rebellion of her day, doing everything she could to flaunt her aunt's lifestyle and convictions. Today she is still a rebellious, depressed individual.

Marlene grew up with the feeling that there was no higher calling in life than to be a wife and mother. When she married David and their two children were born, she felt she was on top of the world. Today, after a decade of marriage, her feelings are persistently misunderstood. David makes no attempt to listen to her point of view or to understand her thoughts. When he isn't preoccupied with work, he sits in his easy chair changing channels on the family's one television from one ball game to another, ignoring his wife's emotional needs, and even what she would enjoy watching. Her feelings? Disillusionment, defeat, despair—and all are manifest in a sloppy house, an unbalanced checkbook, and an unsatisfactory intimate physical relationship.

Sam has worked at a major automotive assembly plant for years. He's had several bosses during that time, all of whom shared one thing in common. They treated their employees like objects. Because of the economy, many of Sam's close friends with whom he has worked have lost their jobs. He has come close to losing his on several occasions. Sam has wanted to change jobs, but because of the economy, he feels caged. He's become burned out, and his careless disregard of company procedures, although subconscious in origin, has led to several incidents of "down time" on the line. Revenge is self-defeating every time.

OBJECTS OF BITTERNESS

SELF

Frequently victims of physical, emotional, or sexual abuse have received a skewed message from their abusers: "I'm no good. I deserve to be trashed." Blaming themselves, they embark on a life of bitter "self-cannibalization."

OTHERS

Perhaps no area of life has generated the degree of bitterness as has the proliferation of divorce. Statistics indicate that one out of two marriages end in divorce. According to *U.S. News and World Report* (October 27, 1986), three out of five children born today will live with a single parent by the age of eighteen. According to a ten-year study by Judith Wallerstein, Executive Director of the Center for the Family in Transition, the impact of divorce on 130 middle class children showed 37 percent of them to experience more emotional trouble five years after the divorce than initially. According to Wallerstein, the subjects in her study "enter relationships with a high level of anxiety and have more trouble with marriage—they want a stable relationship more and are more worried about it than the children of non-divorced parents."

The objects of Wallerstein's study report a high incidence of intense anger and bitterness over the breakup of their homes—even a decade later. Combine the stress of divorce with the trauma of growing up in a single-parent home where children are often expected to take over responsibilities for the absent adult, even to caring for younger siblings, then mix in the trauma of physical, emotional, and sexual abuse, and a residue of intense anger is guaranteed. (A recent study by the University of Michigan Institute for Social Research found that working mothers spent an average of 11 minutes daily in exclusive play time with their kids during weekdays—and only 30 minutes per day on the weekends. For fathers the statistic is even more grim—8 minutes on weekdays, 14 minutes on weekends.)

These circumstances are volatile when combined with high material expectations produced by thousands of hours in front of the television (an average viewing time estimated by the A. C. Nielsen Company is approximately four hours per day), plus the effects of day-care and latchkey kids. It's no wonder that the stresses of childhood frequently lead to unresolved anger and bitterness, which result in burnout in adulthood.

Another factor today is teen pregnancy, or "children having children." For example, Missy is a fourteen-year-old unmarried teenager who lives with her mother, stepfather, and her baby son in a small frame house. Once after her baby was born, Missy admitted to being "sort of mad" about the whole thing. As she puts it, "I didn't want to be pregnant." And the father? "I haven't talked to him recently. He lives in another town. Last time I saw him, he told me he wanted to see the baby when I have it, but I haven't heard from him." Unresolved issues from teenage pregnancy—and the multitude of abortions taking place today—also create a climate in which burnout is likely to proliferate due to unresolved anger issues.

CIRCUMSTANCES

The third object of bitterness may simply be the circumstances that happen in our lives. One festive Friday evening, several hundred people gathered for a party in the atrium lobby of the Kansas City Hyatt Regency Hotel. Hundreds of them lost their lives in an unprecedented disaster when several sky bridges, walkways across the open atrium area, collapsed shortly after seven o'clock. Although the wreckage was cleaned up, many of the injured healed, and the hotel was put back in service, many Kansas City residents, almost a decade later, still can't go near the Hyatt Regency. They have trouble even thinking about the events that took the lives of family or close friends. Many lives are colored permanently by the dark shades of bitterness over disastrous circumstances.

GOD

Whereas many become bitter toward circumstances, others focus their bitterness on God, or at least on their perception of Him. Dianna had set out early in life to make an impact on her generation. Her goal was to enter the field of medicine—perhaps even to be a medical missionary, bringing compassion to some foreign country. Unfortunately, Dianna suffered from several forms of abuse: emotional abuse from her mother (who was herself a victim of abuse), sexual abuse from a youth worker, and ultimately, the trauma of a life-threatening bout with cancer. Dianna finally came to identify herself as an atheist, or at the very least an agnostic. She didn't believe God existed—although, as one compassionate friend frequently pointed out, "You certainly have a lot of anger toward God to really believe He doesn't exist. It seems that if He didn't exist, you wouldn't be nearly so bitter toward Him."

SOME SOLUTIONS FOR BITTERNESS

Although in later chapters we will discuss ways of recovering from burnout, bitterness is so important as a source of burnout we are going to list here some steps you can take to remove bitterness from your life.

REVERSE DENIAL

Face the anger and even the motive for revenge. Recognize the fact that it's gone on too long. Get it out in the open and express it appropriately. Overcoming denial is like going to the dentist. Many of us suggest to the dentist, "Why not skip the injection and the drilling? Just put some of that miraculously hard material over the hole and everything will be OK." But a good dentist knows he has to drill, even when it's painful and that medication is usually necessary in order to dull the pain of drilling to remove the decay.

CHOOSE TO FORGIVE

What is forgiveness? Forgiveness is not treating the offense lightly. It's not pretending that it didn't happen or minimizing the hurt or pain the offense caused. It's not forgetting, because in reality, the events that occurred to us are indelibly recorded in biochemical pathways in the brain. The hurt has become burned into our long-term memory. All we can do is follow the example of Abraham Lincoln who, when confronted with the vindictive actions of one of his political opponents, responded, "I distinctly remember forgetting that."

We can choose to maintain consciousness of harmful events, or we can choose to act as if they had not occurred. Forgiveness is a matter of the will. Furthermore, when we choose to forgive, we relieve a great deal of the ongoing mental and emotional stress that is required for nursing grudges. As a result, we are far less susceptible to burnout.

The word *forgiveness* itself means to send or put away. Forgiveness is the release of a debt. It involves giving up the right to review. It also may involve a continued process. In fact, the process of forgiving is something we often illustrate by describing the peeling of an onion. This illustration is especially appropriate where there has been a great deal of anger and bitterness generated through layer after layer of abuse and hurt. When a person peels an onion, layer after layer becomes visible. When one layer is peeled away, another layer like it can be seen. Each new layer of the onion, when exposed, will likely produce tears—and frequently cause pain, especially if there are scratches and hurts on the person's hands.

If diligence is given to the peeling process, eventually the onion is completely peeled away, layer by layer, until there is no more onion. So it is with bitterness. If we continue to deal with the anger we face each day—the bitterness and anger that come to the surface—eventually we will find that our feelings have been processed to the point of resolution.

Elizabeth was a pastor's wife. For years she gave herself to her husband, her children, and the various churches and individuals to whom they ministered. Over a period of years, the ministry began to take its toll. There were times when her husband was less than sensitive about her physical and emotional needs. Church members were frequently harsh and critical, especially toward her husband and children. Yet many of those same people often demanded hours and hours of her time. Elizabeth soon became burned out.

A change in her husband's schedule, followed by a move to another job, helped some. However, it was not until Elizabeth consciously chose to forgive a number of people—including her husband and children—and expressed a willingness to give up the bitterness that she admitted she felt, that she began to actually recover from burnout. We are far more likely to overcome burnout if we choose to forgive rather than hold on to bitterness.

NEVER TAKE REVENGE

Choose to give up the right to get even. Frequently we encourage people to put this promise into writing. Sandra did so after her husband had become involved with a younger woman at work and she had become clinically depressed. After years of suppressing her rage and bitterness over the infidelity, Sandra, guided by her counselor, wrote out an agreement:

I will no longer remember what I have already acknowledged to have experienced. I have chosen to forgive Bernie this _____ day for what he has done to me. I have measured the size of the pain and acknowledge how much more God has forgiven me. As a result, I hereby agree never to bring up in memory the events that have occurred and to consciously choose to replace thoughts that may come up with thoughts of other subjects. I furthermore give up any right of ever seeking revenge.

It was amazing what a difference that made in Sandra's life. Five years later her marriage—once on the rocks due to the twin threats of her husband's infidelity and her bitterness—is now stronger than ever.

LOOK FOR OPPORTUNITIES TO DO GOOD

Returning a positive word for an insult, doing good when we've been wronged, can disarm the bitterest of enemies. In addition, it can certainly help flush any remains of bitterness from our own lives. Although it involves a choice, an act of the will, it is consistent with love.

RESTORE A SPIRIT OF THANKFULNESS

Since bitterness and gratitude cannot successfully coexist, the more we emphasize the positive things that occur in our lives and focus on them, the more likely we are to eliminate bitterness. Julia, who was mentioned earlier as the individual who had become bitter against the young man she had dated in high school, began keeping a journal. After she processed her bitterness in it, she wrote down at least one positive thing that occurred in her life every day. Whenever she found herself struggling with feelings of bitterness, she would pull out a copy of her journal—she kept a monthly calendar in her purse at all times and stored each month's in a master "catalog of blessings" in her apartment. Reviewing the good things that had happened helped drive feelings of bitterness away.

RENEW YOUR ABILITY TO TRUST PEOPLE

Work on renewing the ability to trust people. When Danny began skiing, he once took a wrong turn on the slopes. Confusing the name of a beginning slope with an advanced downhill run, he went over a mogul—a direct drop-off. His leg was shattered. For a while

Danny considered giving up skiing, even though he had thought he would love it. But a friend who was a veteran skier encouraged him to get back on skis as soon as possible. After his injury had been rehabilitated, Danny soon returned to the slope. It was, in his words, "The most difficult thing I've ever done. I couldn't trust myself. I couldn't trust the ski instructor. When I first started down the hill, I thought I was going to die. But I'm so glad now I did." Danny's renewed trust made the difference.

START LIVING IN THE TODAY

Live life one day at a time. Only by a balanced perspective, resolving the hurt of the past, focusing on the present, and living in confident trust with regard to the future, can an individual overcome the bitterness that lies at the heart of much burnout.

NOTE

1. Les Carter, *Putting the Past Behind* (Chicago: Moody, 1989), p. 43.

6

THE BURNOUT-PRONE PERSONALITY

Several staff members of a college-owned radio station had been working almost nonstop for weeks to develop a multimedia presentation for the college. Hundreds of slides had been taken, processed, selected, and carefully sorted. They had recorded interviews with numerous individuals. Thousands of feet of audiotape had been auditioned and edited. The staff had worked hard to carefully select a wide variety of background music. Finally, all the ingredients were coming together.

As they neared the end of the project, the exhausted crew stopped about three o'clock one afternoon for a quick bite of lunch. Turning to his secretary, the project manager said, "Debi, why don't you ask the blessing on this food."

"Sure," she replied, then quickly prayed, "God, help us to get everything done, now please, and in order. Amen."

The crew broke into laughter.

"What's so funny?" asked the manager.

His administrative assistant replied, "Why, that was the perfect workaholic's prayer. That is *exactly* what you would expect from a group of obsessive-compulsives like us!"

Sometimes being obsessive-compulsive is stimulating, interesting, and a lot of fun. Many times it can be highly productive. Our research at the Minirth-Meier Clinic has shown us that obsessive-compulsive individuals tend to be productive, conscientious workers.

But obsessive-compulsive (perfectionistic) behavior can be destructive, both to obsessive-compulsives and to those around them. Though obsessive-compulsives are unlikely to fail at a job through irresponsibility, carelessness, or neglect, they are inclined to invite disaster by working themselves to the point of burnout. In fact, this book came into existence partially as a result of the harried experience of those radio-station workaholics.

Obsessive-compulsive personality traits can be seen in men and women, college students and farmers, hard driving executives and overstressed housewives.

One such workaholic was Paul Meier. We'll let him tell his own story.

> When I first started my residency in psychiatry at Duke University, I still had a lot of extreme obsessive-compulsive traits, but I had no idea that I was obsessive-compulsive. When I began reading the standard psychiatry textbook on the obsessive-compulsive personality, I carefully studied each page for at least twenty minutes, trying to memorize everything on it.
>
> Two weeks later, I had covered only about forty pages when I read that obsessive-compulsives seldom finish a book. They accumulate a lot of books, but they seldom finish reading one, because they spend so much time poring over each page, trying to memorize everything. Suddenly that information hit me between the eyes. I had to admit that I had all the traits I had been reading about for the past two weeks. That made me so angry that I slammed the book shut. And to this day I haven't finished reading it.

Even though most obsessive-compulsives stress the importance of objective thinking, they often find it hard to take an objective look at themselves. Paul Meier is not the only "O-C" ever to have difficulty identifying the strengths and weaknesses in his own personality.

WHO IS THE OBSESSIVE-COMPULSIVE?

What is the origin of the term *obsessive-compulsive?* Clinically speaking, an obsession is a particular thought repeated over and over to the point that it is difficult to dislodge from the mind. Such *obsessions* usually result in frequently repeated behavior patterns. Those are known as *compulsions.*

Obsessive-compulsives come in all shapes and sizes and manifest all degrees of behavior. In its extreme, obsessive-compulsive behavior takes the form of agoraphobia (a fear of open places), panic attacks, anxiety attacks, an inability to sleep, and sometimes even difficulty in functioning at all. If the latter occurs, the obsessive-compulsive individual may need to be hospitalized or receive intensive insight-oriented counseling to discover the root cause of the obsession and the resulting compulsions.

Needless to say, most obsessive-compulsives don't go nearly that far. Examples of relatively normal obsessive-compulsive behavior include the man who frequently pats his hip pocket to see if his wallet is still there, the housewife who calls her husband's office three times to remind him to get home early to visit with his in-laws, and the football coach who watches the preceding week's game film twenty times, trying to find clues to reverse his team's three-game losing streak. And as you can see, obsessive-compulsive behavior isn't necessarily negative.

Dr. Frank Minirth, who admits to being "O-C," has developed a 129-point list describing the major characteristics of the obsessive-compulsive personality trait. Particularly significant is item number 128. It reads "The obsessive-compulsive likes lists."

The following test of obsessive-compulsive behavior helps us to get to know the O-C a little better.

1. An O-C will figure out a numbering system for almost anything, from wardrobe planning to reading all the research papers in his chosen field. He is especially O-C if he writes research papers.

2. He takes intensive notes in his devotional time. He is especially O-C if he periodically rereads those notes.

3. He takes psychological testing each year just to see if he has grown more obsessive-compulsive.

4. He averaged more than forty pages of class notes for each high school, college, or graduate class. He is especially O-C if he invested the time to type up those notes.

5. He always makes it a point to arrive within sixty seconds of the exact time of an appointment. He is especially O-C if he becomes significantly depressed when he is unable to fulfill that commitment.

6. He makes extensive lists of things to do. He is especially O-C if he categorizes his lists on carefully filed three-by-five-inch index cards.

7. He feels a desperate need to reorganize his filing system several times a year.

8. He keeps his checkbook balanced—to the penny. If he finds that impossible, he may postpone examining his checkbook figures at all.

9. If he takes a psychological stress test, he will regularly score in the top 5 percentile.

10. He constantly finds himself trying to do two things at once. He dictates letters into a cassette recorder as he drives through rush-hour traffic on a suburban expressway, or writes a research paper on a flight from Tampa to Dallas—at the same time he eats a snack.

11. He finds himself saying, "I'll do it myself, and I'll do it right." If he is blessed with a "Type A personality" as well—with its chronic competitiveness, high achievement orientation, and impatience—he will add, "Right now!"

12. He checks the time more than twice an hour. He is especially O-C if he does this on his day off.

13. He eats while he works. He is especially O-C if he snarfs a granola bar in the elevator, or a Big Mac in rush-hour traffic.

14. He wants to name his children alphabetically from oldest to youngest. He is especially O-C if he wants to alliterate all their names.

If you can identify with a majority of those traits, then the person gazing back at you from the mirror is probably a certified obsessive-compulsive.

HARRY AND JULIE

In college Harry wanted to participate in almost every campus activity. He played on the basketball and the baseball teams, became active in several campus organizations, joined the debate team, sang in a choir, took every possible elective course, dated every weekend, and even managed a small business on the side. When Harry finished college, his grade point average hardly reflected his intelligence level. In high school he had been able to keep up his grade level while carrying on numerous outside activities. Too late he discovered that high intelligence alone wasn't enough to ensure his success in college. That would have required that he spend a good deal of time on one goal alone—his studies.

Julie was in college with Harry. Her grades were good. Whenever Julie worked on an assignment, she'd spend hours on background research. She was never satisfied that she'd done enough. When she typed a paper, it had to be letter perfect. Indeed, typing caused her great anxiety and distraction, for each page had to be error-free. If it wasn't, she'd redo the whole page.

But Julie found that her O-C behavior limited her overall college experience. She spent a great deal of her time tidying up her dormitory room and doing her laundry. She shied away from most of the extracurricular campus activities, and as a result met few people except at church on Sundays. Even then she barely became acquainted, for she didn't have much experience in developing close friendships. Julie didn't see the big picture of how other college activities could develop the interpersonal skills she would need throughout her life.

Believe it or not, Julie and Harry were not personality opposites. Instead, both of them had obsessive-compulsive personality traits, the main one being a desire to exhibit "perfect" behavior to prove one's personal worth. They both experienced anxiety about not being accepted, about not being good enough.

Their personalities looked different because they defined "being good enough" from opposite points of the spectrum. Harry defined it *quantitatively*. His biggest worry was that he might not be participating in enough activities in college. Julie defined "being good enough" *qualitatively*. Her biggest concern was that she might not be doing any one thing well enough. Not surprisingly, though they came from opposite extremes, they shared a difficulty in managing their time. Neither had achieved balance in the way they regarded and used time.

Put another way, Julie was a *quality* perfectionist and Harry a *quantity* perfectionist. Julie's obsessive-compulsive extremes were mixed with some passive-aggressive behavior. She felt aggression toward doing what she felt she "ought" to do, so she showed that aggression passively by dragging her feet when she worked on a project she thought she should complete. Because she was also obsessive-compulsive and thought that everything should be done perfectly, the two personality traits fed upon one another.

Julie took a long time to complete her projects because she could not easily accept her work as good enough to consider any one job completed. In addition, drawing out a project allowed her to act out her negative feelings toward "oughtness" or authority through passivity, that is, by taking longer than necessary to complete what she thought she *should* do.

Harry's Type A behavior (see the Glossary and chapter 10 for more about the Type A) consisted of O-C tendencies combined with hysteric or histrionic behavior. He was excessively competitive and highly achievement oriented, as long as others could see and appreciate those achievements. He suffered from a chronic sense of pressure and often was impatient with the pace of life. He wanted to prove to the whole world how good he was at what he did—and how quickly he could do it.

The quantity perfectionist is the one who gives himself twenty things to do in a day, completes nineteen, and then wants to kick himself that night for not getting the twentieth task done. He is frequently a firstborn child.

And he does not simply want to do many things. He wants to do many things at once—without concentrating on doing as thorough a job as he might. He wants to please or to win approval from everybody—to have everyone's attention and applause. That can best be done, he thinks, by a flurry of activity, not by doing one thing well. To the Type A obsessive-compulsive, more is better and most is best.

Traditional obsessive-compulsives like Julie usually zero in on accomplishing one thing absolutely perfectly. But they cannot decide what is absolute perfection, so they never consider a project completed, for there might still be some way it could be further improved. An only child, or the only boy or the only girl in a family, tends to have the combination of O-C and passive-aggressive traits that define this kind of quality perfectionism. Such a child is likely to have had perfectionistic parents who did his thinking for him—and who made most of his decisions.

As a consequence, the child has strong obedience-defiance conflicts. Part of him really does want to please the authority figures in his life. So he strives to do what he thinks will please his parents and at the same time bring himself personal satisfaction. Yet all the while, he resents the perceived demands of authority figures. So in an unconscious resort to rebellion and vengeance, he acts passively by never actually finishing those tasks that he thinks would be pleasing to those authority figures.

THE PROBLEM OF TIME

Obsessive-compulsives tend to take an extreme approach to time. Type A people easily become slaves to the clock. They are constantly looking at their watches, checking calendars, reviewing their daily diaries and lists of things to do, crossing off this and adding that, and endeavoring in every way to cram more and more into less and less time. Evidence that a Type A mentality is flourishing in today's society can be seen in the success of such books as *The One-Minute Manager, The One-Minute Mother,* and *The One-Minute Father.* Each of those books contains simple, easy-to-use principles for dealing with relationships in the workplace or the home. Our purpose is not to criticize such books. They contain much that is useful. But built into the concept of the one-minute person is the principle that it is possible to do more in less time, a major preoccupation of the Type A obsessive-compulsive. Yet even *The One-Minute Father* recognizes that "these . . . methods of personal communication with your children are just a slice of the parenting pie. Being a good parent takes a good deal more than spending a minute now and then with your children."[1]

Contrast the one-minute mentality with the mind-set of the founder of the Procrastinator's Club of America, Les Waas. He believes that the people who fail to relax are the people who die early. So he doesn't mind if you refer to him as the "late" Mr. Waas. In fact, the slogan for his organization is "Procrastinate Now." Procrastinators such as Mr. Waas tend to be basically passive-aggressive, and their approach to any deadline is "There's always tomorrow."

The basic obsessive-compulsive usually has some passive-aggressive traits. Though he may be more conscientious than the basic passive-aggressive person, his personality still leans toward the Procrastinator's Club thinking—that of wanting to rebel against time and deadlines, even reasonable ones.

At the heart of both Harry's and Julie's problems was an inability to focus on what was truly important. Both filled up their days with activity, but neither used time strategically. Harry ran from activity to activity, while Julie methodically perfected each detail of the tasks she attempted. Yet neither achieved a balance of emphasis (focusing one's time strategically) and breadth (participating in a variety of activities) in his total college experience. To do that they would have had to balance the extremes of quality and quantity, something neither one could do.

NOTE

1. Spencer Johnson, *The One-Minute Father* (New York: Morrow, 1983), p. 99.

7

THE WORKAHOLIC
AND HIS WORKPLACE

When most people hear the word *burnout,* they think of the hard-driving business person who never stops for coffee breaks or relaxing lunches and insists on taking work home at night, or even on vacations. There are, of course, occasional situations where such a work style is necessary. If those habits have been practiced long-term, however, their necessity is as much in the mind of the workaholic as in the reality of the situation.

Seemingly logical explanations of "That's the only way to get the job done," "That's the only way to get ahead in my profession (or company)," or "We need the extra money," are all too often cover-ups for the feeling "That's the only way to prove to them what I'm worth," which ties in with the feeling "That's the only way to prove to myself and others what I'm worth."

Many times a workaholic will try to make a virtue out of his overdependence on work (for a feeling of self-worth) by exalting work, the Protestant work ethic, and even capitalism to a very high plane. All three are good in moderation, but they do not excuse destructive workaholic habits. Workaholism for the purpose of glorifying or exalting self is both unnecessary and wrong.

WORKAHOLISM AND GUILT

To verify the rightness of their workaholic tendencies, strong obsessive-compulsive individuals point out that whenever they slow down, they feel guilty for not accomplishing all that they *should* be doing, or even all that they believe they have the ability to accomplish. Yet, we shouldn't carry out work that causes us to neglect our families and our health.

The unnecessary guilt, or false guilt, that workaholics feel whenever they slow down, may be related to an anxiety regarding their fear of facing what they did not accomplish during their times of frenetic workaholic activity—things such as spending time with their family or improving their own mental and physical health. Also, many of the accomplishments of workaholics are found later to be for nothing, because not enough time was spent in planning and prioritizing for long-term accomplishment. To the workaholic, everything seems extremely important and urgent all the time.

One burnout victim, the president of a fairly large company, told us of his harsh realization that all his work created an imbalance with his family life. Allowing himself to become one-dimensional and obsessed with work, even to the detriment of everything else in his life, had seemed to be a good quality previously. Now he had begun to see it for the selfishness it was.

That executive's personality, like that of all workaholics, was loaded with obsessive-compulsive personality traits, some good and some bad.

To discover whether or not your personality is primarily obsessive-compulsive, which may mean you are susceptible to workaholism and eventual burnout, check to see if a majority of the following traits apply to you.

OBSESSIVE-COMPULSIVE PERSONALITY TRAITS

The obsessive-compulsive

1. is perfectionistic, neat, clean, orderly, dutiful, conscientious, meticulous, and moral
2. does a good job but works too hard and is unable to relax
3. is choleric, overly conscientious, overly concerned, inflexible, has an overly strict conscience and rigid thinking
4. rationalizes to deceive and defend self and intellectualizes in order to avoid emotions
5. is a good student, well-organized, and interested in facts, not feelings; seems cold and stable and tends to split hairs
6. is antiauthority at times and is pulled between actions of obedience and defiance; obedience usually wins, but occa-

sionally defiance wins. Obedience leads to rage, and the defiance leads to fear; the fear leads to perfectionistic traits, whereas the rage leads to nonperfectionistic traits; a basic problem is defiant anger

7. displays many opposite traits: conscientiousness and negligence, orderliness and untidiness

8. has three central concerns: dirt (he or she is very clean), time (he or she is punctual), and money (he or she wants a feeling of financial security)

9. has feelings of helplessness, needs to be in control of self and others who are close to him or her, needs power, and is intensely competitive

10. keeps emotions a secret from others, feels with the mind (is too logical) and, as a defense, isolates feelings from whatever he or she is experiencing

11. uses other defenses, including *magical thinking*—thinking he or she has more power than reality dictates; *reaction formation*—adopting attitudes and behavior that are opposite to the impulses the individual consciously or unconsciously harbors; and *undoing*—unconsciously acting out in reverse some unacceptable action that occurred in the past

12. struggles to bring conversations around to the level of theories

13. is afraid of feelings of warmth (which occurred in dependent relationships in early life), expresses anger more easily (because it encourages distance), postpones pleasure (out of unconscious guilt), lives in the future, lacks spontaneity, and is insecure

14. may have unspontaneous and routine sex with little variety; female perfectionists have difficulty with orgasm, and male perfectionists sometimes have difficulty with premature ejaculation; both symptoms are a result of anxiety, which is related to the obsessive-compulsive's fear of loss of control

15. usually had a parent or parents who were obsessive and demanded total devotion but gave minimal love, and who made the person feel accepted on a conditional basis (only when doing what the parent wanted him or her to do)

16. needs respect and security

17. craves dependent relationships but fears them at the same time
18. needs to feel omnipotent; substitutes feelings of omnipotence for true coping
19. has trouble with commitment, fears loss of control, often focuses on irrelevant details
20. frequently uses techniques to conceal anger, such as shaking hands with a handshake that is rigid
21. has feelings of powerlessness and avoids recognition of personal fallibility; fears the possibility of being proved wrong and lives in much doubt about personal words and actions; checks and rechecks door latches to achieve certainty and security
22. is extraordinarily self-willed, uses his or her defense mechanisms to control aggressive impulses, and avoids real conflicts by dwelling on substitute obsessive thoughts (if those defense mechanisms do not work, the result is often depression)
23. is stubborn, stingy (with love and time), frugal, persistent, dependable in many ways, and reliable
24. has an overdeveloped superego, feels comfortable only when knowing everything, and tends to insist on ultimate truth in all matters
25. has exaggerated expectations of self and others

(Our alcohol-rehabilitation counselor from chapter 3, Lewis, was just such a person. He expected to cure his alcoholic patients, and he expected them to do what was necessary to be cured. When that didn't happen, he had to admit that he wasn't perfect, which to him was to be contemptible. He received some psychiatric help, quit drinking himself (following his own advice), and resolved his anger and frustrations. He came to realize that when dealing with alcoholics, you need to recognize that some of them will respond and want to get over their problem and will do very well, and some of them will not.

Lewis came to accept his limitations and realized that the responsibility for his patients' recovery was on their shoulders, not his. His responsibility was to point out to them what they needed to do and then to leave it up to them whether or not to work out their problems. As a result, Lewis returned to his work and was able to function well without feeling burned out.)

26. appears strong, decisive, and affirmative, but is not; rather, he or she is uncertain, uneasy, and wavering; follows rules rigidly to control uncertainty; needs to appear perfect

27. exaggerates the power of personal thoughts; substitutes words (spoken or unspoken) for responsible action

28. has a grandiose self-view and strives to accomplish superhuman achievements to overcome insecurities; accepting his or her own limitations amounts to being average— which is contemptible

    (Our case example Ellen, the mother who felt overly responsible when a child rebelled, had just such a grandiose self-view. She thought the success of her children depended upon her alone. When one child rebelled, she not only blamed herself but saw herself as a less than perfect mother, one with limitations and therefore contemptible. That self-view brought on depression and burnout. She didn't realize that every child will make mistakes and that all parents make mistakes in parenting. Ellen was encouraged by our staff to quit carrying all the guilt and blame for her child's wrong choices. That is not to say that parents should overlook their parenting mistakes. They should ask for forgiveness for their mistakes and love their children unconditionally. Then they need to turn the responsibility for their grown children's future success over to their child.)

29. is cautious in love relationships, because love results in concern about another's feelings that are not under one's own control

30. has a single-minded style of thinking, is good at tasks that require intense concentration, and believes that everything is either black or white, completely right or completely wrong

31. has a tendency to overrespond

32. is critical, but cannot stand criticism

33. has strong rituals in his or her personal religious system; considers rituals important in many other areas of life

34. considers commitment tantamount to dependency and being out of control; finds marriage commitment difficult —prefers coexistence
35. lives in the future, saves for a tomorrow that never arrives, discounts limitations of time, and denies death
36. insists on honesty in marriage, which results in telling all at times
37. has trouble admitting mistakes
38. uses excessive cautions or restraints in courtship
39. gives minimal commitment in relationships but demands maximal commitment (As a result, each marriage partner pursues his own interests and intimacy is limited; he or she is careful to do only a minimal share in marriage but wants to *think* for both self and spouse.)
40. is legalistic with himself and others
41. is (1) *pecuniary*—obsessed with money matters, (2) *parsimonious*—frugal or stingy, and (3) *pedantic*—overly concerned with book knowledge and formal rules

THE WORKAHOLIC'S INNER VOICES

Inner "voices" or convictions are what keep workaholics going. They tell workaholics, who are usually the oldest children of their sex in the family, that they need to *do* something to *be* worthwhile. Those voices or convictions do not let him or her rest in just being someone. "Doing" is the key to being worthwhile. The cause usually lies in unrealistic expectations for a first child by parents who try to get the child to do or accomplish new activities before a child could normally accomplish them. That is partly out of anxiety—to be sure the child is normal—and partly out of parental pride, to improve their own self-esteem through raising an above-normal child. By the time a second child comes along, those desires and anxieties have been somewhat satisfied and the parents are more realistic about what to expect from a child at different stages. Meanwhile, that first child grows up following inner voices that drive him on.

VOICE FROM CHILDHOOD

That unhealthy voice or driving message says, "You're a nobody. What can you do to prove you're a somebody?" When the workaholic starts to do something to prove self-worth, the voice says, "Keep doing more, more." When the workaholic reaches a goal, the voice says, "That's good, but it's not enough." Workaholics never reach the point of doing enough to prove that self is a "somebody" and relax in that knowledge. The only way workaholics (or anyone else, for that matter) can truly prove they are somebodies is to accept the fact that others see them as somebodies. True self-worth can be experienced only as we understand and acknowledge our position in this way.

VOICE OF THE SELF-CENTERED SELF

That voice says, "I'll do what I want to do. I'll have fun or do my own thing." That conviction comes into dominance when the workaholic gives up on the first voice in exhaustion—in other words when he is approaching burnout. The burned-out workaholic may still be going to work in order to receive a paycheck, but he or she is no longer exerting as much effort as usual.

VOICE OF COLLEAGUES

Another inner voice, also unhealthy, says, "Don't take time off; you can't afford it. People won't understand." Actually, that voice may not represent the actual thoughts of the workaholic's colleagues but what he or she assumes colleagues would say. To overcome that voice, the workaholic must consider what are his or her actual priorities in life and in the particular task at hand. When new therapists are hired at the Minirth-Meier Clinic, we caution them (1) that the number of cases they have affects the profit the clinic makes, as well as their own salary, but (2) if their caseload becomes so heavy that it affects their home life, they are to call a halt to accepting new cases. Those priorities must be recognized and followed in the daily routine.

VOICE OF REALITY

Another voice that all of us hear at times is the voice of reality, a healthy voice that we all need. That voice tells us to "face the music" and realize that mounting debt or some other problem means that we will need to work harder or longer for a particular period of time.

When that period of time is up, however, we will again need to slow down to a normal pace. The problem with workaholics, however, is that when a crisis is over they keep finding more reasons to continue the extra exertion and long hours.

TYPICAL VIEWPOINTS OF THE WORKAHOLIC

- *I think that the people I know who are in authority are no better than I am.*

Burnout includes an underlying cynical attitude and a rebellion against authority figures. That attitude revolves around one's expectations not being met.

- *Once I start a job, I have no peace until I finish it.*

If you work day and night until you finish a job, it not only shows that work comes before everything else but may be related to authority rebellion as well. It could be tied in with an attitude that says, "I'll show him!" or with frustration because a boss has set unrealistic time limits and demands. It may also be tied in with an idea that "If I can just get that project put into a nice, neat little package, it will show him (and me) that I'm a worthwhile person."

- *I like to tell people exactly what I think.*

As workaholics become burned out, they become irritable and likely to say anything without holding back, because so much emotion is pent up inside that there is no room to store more. Also, the more burned out they are, the more omnipotent and right they feel about personal viewpoints. As insecurity about decreasing abilities mounts, the victim becomes more arrogant. "I am right and everyone else is wrong!"

- *Although many people are overly conscious of feelings, I like to deal only with the facts.*

If you take the emotional part of a workaholic's personality away, you would notice no difference. A workaholic represses feelings (except for irritability, and he or she doesn't recognize the basis for the irritability).

We often give the following inventory to suspected workaholic patients. Complete it as quickly as possible.[1] Your first response is often your most honest answer. If you have been wondering about your own tendencies toward workaholic burnout, see how many of these statements you agree with and add one example or comment. True or false:

CHECKLIST FOR WORKAHOLIC BURNOUT

1. I feel that the people I know who are in authority are no better than I am.

2. Once I start a job, I have no peace until I finish it.

3. I like to tell people exactly what I think.

4. Although many people are overly conscious of feelings, I like to deal only with the facts.

5. I worry a lot about business and financial matters.

6. I often have anxiety about something or someone.

7. I sometimes become so preoccupied by a thought that I cannot get it out of my mind.

8. I find it difficult to go to bed or sleep because of thoughts bothering me.

9. I have periods during which I cannot sit or lie down because I need to be doing something.

10. My mind is often occupied by thoughts about what I have done wrong or not completed.

11. My concentration is not what it used to be.

12. My personal appearance is almost always neat and clean.

13. I feel irritated when I see another person's messy desk or cluttered room.

14. I am more comfortable in a neat, clean, and orderly room than in a messy one.

15. I cannot get through a day or a week without a schedule or a list of jobs to do.

16. I believe that the man who works the hardest and longest deserves to get ahead.

17. If my job/housework demands more time, I will cut out pleasurable activities to see that it gets done.

18. My conscience often bothers me about things I have done in the past.

19. There are things that I have done that would embarrass me greatly if they become public knowledge.

20. When I was a student I felt uncomfortable unless I got the highest grade.

21. It is my view that many people become confused because they don't bother to find out all the facts.

22. I frequently feel angry without knowing what or who is bothering me.

23. I can't stand to have my checkbook or financial matters out of balance.

24. I think talking about feelings to others is a waste of time.

25. There have been times when I became preoccupied with washing my hands or keeping things clean.

26. I like always to be in control of myself and to know as much as possible about things happening around me.

27. I have few or no close friends with whom I share warm feelings openly.

28. I feel that the more one can know about future events, the better off he will be.

29. There are sins I have committed that I will never live down.

30. I always avoid being late to a meeting or an appointment.

31. I rarely give up until a job has been completely finished.

32. I often expect things of myself that no one else would ask.

33. I sometimes worry about whether I was wrong or made a mistake.

34. I would like others to see me as not having any faults.

35. The groups and organizations I join have strict rules and regulations.

36. I believe we have commands and rules to live by, and we fail if we don't follow all of them.

Now go back and count the number of statements you answered "true." A score of 10 or less reflects a fairly relaxed person. A score of 11 to 20 is average. A score of 21 or more reflects a definite tendency toward workaholism. If you scored in the twenties or beyond, you are also likely to become a victim of burnout.

LOOKING FOR EMPLOYEE BURNOUT

An employer or supervisor may suspect burnout when an employee exhibits frequent absenteeism, indecision, and little attention to personal grooming and health. The Monday "blahs" or blues may be an indication of approaching burnout. Of course, by the time the Monday "blahs" last all week, the employee is in the midst of burnout. If the burnout victim is a supervisor, he or she should realize that burnout symptoms probably exist in those that report to him or her, as well. The supervisor should consider what can be done to encourage employees to want to come to work. It may include changes in reporting relationships, in office environment, and in allowing employees to have a say in the best way to accomplish projects.

Often the relationship between employee and supervisor is to blame for burnout. As for our nurse case example, Anne (who was working too much overtime and was ignoring patients' buzzers), therapy helped her get in touch with the anger she felt toward her supervisor. After that she was able to become helpfully assertive without fearing her supervisor's wrath or power. She let her supervisor know that she could not function if she continued working that many hours. Anne told her that she either had to work a forty-hour week or find another job, and her supervisor agreed to allow her to work a reduced schedule. Through therapy, learning to forgive her supervisor, and cutting down her work schedule, Anne was able to overcome her burnout and return to her previous role in the healing of her patients.

One area of burnout experienced by many people today is that involving the start of a new business venture. Often a new entrepreneur will work day and night to make a new venture profitable in a shorter amount of time than is necessary. The time constraint usually has to do with financial considerations. Not enough money was available at the beginning of the venture to keep it afloat for the amount of time needed to start turning a profit. A word of warning might be to make sure enough money has been saved or raised before entering a new venture, rather than burning yourself out trying to make the new venture profitable in a short time.

PRIORITIES FOR THE WORKAHOLIC

The crux of the consideration for those who don't want to burn out may be to consider whether they are in the job that is right for them. If you think you will really be fired if you spend sufficient time with family and on rest and relaxation, then it is unlikely that that job is for you. Before quitting the company, however, it may be fruitful to investigate whether there is another type of position in the same company that would suit you better.

One young accountant in a large company realized that his chosen career was giving him little opportunity to deal with people on a personal level. Because he needed such contact, he asked to be switched to the human relations, or personnel, department of the company as a trainer. Today he has won numerous awards for his innovative work-efficiency programs and methods of motivating factory workers.

If you quit the road to burnout, you may indeed face the possibility of being fired. However, you may be surprised to find that your rating in the company will go up instead of down, as you enter each day more fresh and ready to give your best to producing during the part of the day that should be allotted to work.

One former burnout victim and workaholic, a company CEO, uses the following checklist to get his life in balance:

1. Realize that you don't have to be perfect to be somebody. You are already somebody.

2. Realize that you don't have to be completely neat in order to have other people, or yourself, approve of you.

3. Look at life from the eternity perspective. What will you take with you? As has often been said, you won't see a hearse pulling a U-Haul trailer.

4. Learn to relax with activities that are relaxing to you.

5. Get in touch with your hidden anger, then forgive others for their part in it, and forgive yourself for having it.

Learning a new way of life comes hard for the workaholic, but it is necessary. A workaholic has to practice being relaxed, practice saying no to others' expectations of him, schedule time for spiritual exercises, schedule eight hours of sleep, and schedule time with family. The alternative is to become progressively less productive and of less benefit to loved ones and to himself as a result of burnout.

NOTE

1. Presented first in *The Workaholic and His Family,* by Frank Minirth et al. (Grand Rapids: Baker, 1981), pp. 23-26.

8
MORE CHARACTERISTICS
OF O-Cs

Recently one of us was speaking at a conference in a western state. During the conference he stayed in the home of a staff member of a particular organization. One evening his hostess stated rather strongly, "I am really not sure I agree with all of what you said about obsessive-compulsive behavior or workaholism. In fact, I don't like it."

"Really?" the author replied. "Tell me why."

"I just think those things don't apply to me."

"Tell me a little about yourself," the speaker replied.

"Well, I am certainly not obsessive-compulsive or a workaholic," she said. "However, my dad certainly was. He was an extremely critical, highly demanding, hard-working businessman, and he expected a lot out of us. In fact, I decided early in life that I would make it a point not to be at all like my father."

It's not hard to imagine the direction the conversation took. Within half an hour the housewife reluctantly began to admit that she had a number of obsessive-compulsive personality traits—characteristics she had sought to suppress or deny for years. Finally, she threw up her hands. "I guess the reason I didn't like what you were saying is that it described me perfectly. I must have caught my father's obsessive-compulsive behavior after all."

However, being an obsessive-compulsive is not a "caught" behavior. And there is no evidence that O-C traits are hereditary. Psychological studies indicate that the primary factor is one's early environment. Many of those studies indicate that the majority of our personality traits are formed prior to our sixth birthday and certainly by the time we become teenagers.

Most individuals with a high number of obsessive-compulsive traits have parents who were also obsessive. A person is especially likely to become O-C if the parent of the opposite sex was extremely strict, demanded complete devotion and total obedience, and gave a minimal amount of attention—love, affection, hugs, or positive strokes. To such a parent, everything was either black or white. The child was either a success or a failure. So the child felt accepted on a conditional basis. That conditional love led to the child's need to achieve or to perform to get the parent's approval.

As one highly motivated obsessive-compulsive told her counselor, "Dad was very successful in his business, but he wasn't very good at relating to my mother or to us children. He always expected us to be the best, but he never seemed to think that we could do anything. Whether it was chores around the house, helping him with his business, or doing things at school, we had to be perfect." When asked if her father had ever told her that he loved her, her quick reply was, "No, never. Not until I was grown and out of the house."

"Did he give you lots of hugs when you were growing up?"

"No, he wasn't affectionate at all."

This daughter, like many obsessive-compulsives, attempted superhuman achievements to try to overcome her feelings of uncertainty that conditional love had produced.

Describing the workaholic, obsessive-compulsive father in the *Wall Street Journal* (April 6, 1981), Sanford L. Jacobs wrote, "He gets home long after the children have eaten. She [the wife] used to eat with them but now she waits for her husband. Usually the children have gone to bed by then. One child asked recently, 'Isn't Daddy going to be home again tonight?'"

Two possible consequences of obsessive-compulsive, workaholic behavior in parents are: (1) a child acts out, telling the parent to "buzz off," and (2) the oldest child develops an intense motivation to strive after achievements to try to win the workaholic or obsessive-compulsive parent's approval.

TRAITS OF PARENTS OF OBSESSIVE-COMPULSIVES

Another common characteristic of the obsessive-compulsive is that he gives himself and others a highly disproportionate number of "should," "ought," or "must" messages. Although clear parental direction is extremely important for children, constantly hearing "shoulds," "oughts," or "musts" leads them to believe that if they don't perform, they aren't worthy. That message, reinforced throughout childhood, produces many second-generation obsessive-compulsives. A number of psychological studies reveal the following list of traits found in parents of obsessive-compulsives:

- *They spend a great amount of time talking to their children but very little time listening.*

Most of their talk centers on commands, instructions, criticisms, and the previously discussed "should" messages.

- *Obsessive-compulsive parents have a tendency to expect perfect manners, even at an early age.*

One particularly obsessive-compulsive couple pushed their children into church each Sunday and seated them in descending order from the oldest to the youngest. They wouldn't allow even a wiggle out of the two year old. Obsessive-compulsive parents don't tolerate mistakes, not even a small amount of spilled milk.

- *Obsessive-compulsives tend to be extremely critical of other people, especially in front of their children.*

Many of them practice snobbery, often putting down others. By the same token, these obsessive-compulsives often have friends who are introverts and seldom allow their children to interact openly with other people.

- *Obsessive-compulsive parents have a tendency to emphasize the letter of the law, sometimes to the extent of practicing hypocrisy.*

Emphasizing the Victorian ethic, they tend to communicate to their children the view that high moral standards demonstrate personal superiority and can even contribute toward earning one's way to heaven. However, despite personal rigidity and "no exception" rules, obsessive-compulsive parents frequently avoid any serious personal commitment to these rules. Their commitment is on the surface.

- *Obsessive-compulsive parents are usually extremely critical of the material convictions of the child's grandparents, which they characterize as miserly.*

The grandparents may have resented even normal childhood expenses when raising the parents—school fees, allowances, new shoes and clothes for rapidly growing children. As a result, the second generation of O-Cs often develops a personal preoccupation with money and communicates a materialistic mind-set to their own children, the third generation.

Surprisingly, materialistic thinking cuts across economic levels. It can be seen in children of multimillionaires and poverty-level missionaries alike. In the case of one family whose income was well below the poverty level, the parents constantly communicated a resentment about the things they didn't have.

Not surprisingly, several of the children dedicated themselves to earning large sums of money and, in the process, became obsessive-compulsive workaholics.

- *Obsessive-compulsive parents outwardly communicate that the father is the boss; however, the children soon learn that he is just a figurehead.*

The mother is actually the dominating force in the family. One obsessive-compulsive observed rather caustically, "My dad was sort of a cross between Archie Bunker and Jackie Gleason's Ralph of 'The Honeymooners.' He went around thumping his chest saying, 'I am the king of this castle.' But in reality we knew that Mother was in charge."

Those are just a few of the traits we've observed in the parents of obsessive-compulsive workaholics.

We have also observed that it is most common for a firstborn child, regardless of his parents' personality types, to become obsessive-compulsive. Perhaps the reason is that new parents tend to expect a lot from themselves as parents and a lot from their children. As a result, they tend to be harder on their firstborn. Because they are more uptight about the process of parenting, they don't allow themselves room for error. Consequently, they cannot handle mistakes in their children because they see those mistakes as reflections on their own parental abilities. In most instances, by the time the next child arrives on the scene, the parents have mellowed in their approach to parenting. Thus, second children tend to have more problems with competing for attention than with striving for perfection. They tend to develop histrionic (or hysteric) personalities, which are emotional, excitable, overly dramatic, self-centered, manipulative, and naive. By the time the final child arrives, the parents hate to give up their controlling influence in the child's life. They tend to pamper and baby the youngest, turning that child into a passive-dependent or passive-aggressive personality who expects other people (first parents, later others) to fight all his or her battles in life.

Obviously these general principles have exceptions. However, if you are aware of the ways in which your obsessive-compulsive personality was produced, then you may be able to avoid pushing your own children too far down that same road.

O-C PERSONALITY TRAITS

On first impression, the obsessive-compulsive seems to be a conscientious and dutiful individual, highly obedience-oriented. He is likely to be a hard worker (usually working too hard), has a strict conscience, and is highly motivated. As one hard-working O-C frequently told his children, "Work makes life sweet." The O-C tends to be self-sacrificing and more willing to give up personal gain or desires than some other personality types that lean toward more selfish behavior.

One of the results of such self-sacrificing behavior is that obsessive-compulsives tend to be extremely successful. Statistically, obsessive-compulsive personalities in mid- to upper-level management positions in American business and industry are outnumbered only by paranoid personality types. Paranoid personalities are afraid of other people's controlling them, so they strive to take control themselves.

When taken alone, the obsessive-compulsive traits described above give the impression that the obsessive-compulsive personality type is the most desirable one to have. We know, however, that people aren't all alike. We are equally important and interdependent on one another. We need, therefore, to recognize the importance of the personable hysteric (or histrionic), the sensitive paranoid, the servant-hearted passive, the highly energetic cyclothymic, and other personalities.

We must also recognize that some negative traits may overshadow the positive aspects of the obsessive-compulsive personality. Most obsessives are aware of those negative traits but tend to deny them, since denial is one of the chief defense mechanisms (reactive behaviors) people employ to cope with the anxiety they would feel if they were fully aware of their selfish emotions.

ADDITIONAL EXTREME TENDENCIES

The obsessive-compulsive personality is also likely to possess the following extreme characteristics.

PERFECTIONISTIC

A perfectionist has a tendency to expect himself to be perfect all the time. He becomes intensely angry with himself when he demonstrates such imperfections as losing his car keys, forgetting his checkbook, or even failing to keep his checkbook balanced. If an obsessive-compulsive homemaker fails to take care of all her children perfectly, she may become very depressed.

Furthermore, perfectionistic obsessive-compulsives tend to expect perfection from others. This can create chaos in marital and work relationships, and even may produce a generation of highly perfectionistic, workaholic, obsessive-compulsive children.

DETAIL-ORIENTED

Obsessive-compulsives often develop a meticulous concern for detail. They frequently labor far too hard on a given project. In fact, one obsessive author we know, writing a voluminous book, spent many months writing and rewriting the first three chapters, unable to go on to chapter 4, because the first three "just aren't perfect yet." As perfectionists drive themselves to the limit, they are frequently unable or, more accurately, *unwilling*, to relax. Obsessive-compulsives become overly concerned about every detail. They are strong in organization but may spend more time getting organized than they spend on just about anything else.

They have a tendency to focus on the future and have a great deal of difficulty relaxing and enjoying life in the present. Obsessives are the kind of individuals who, when eating a hot fudge sundae, save what they consider the best part, the maraschino cherry on top of the whipped cream, for last. Or, after considering the amount of number 2 red dye contained in that topping, they refuse to eat the cherry at all!

PROJECT-DIRECTED

Obsessive-compulsives tend to focus on projects rather than on people. That tendency is undergirded by an orientation toward facts rather than feelings. Psychiatric research has long demonstrated that the left side of the human brain is used for processing factual or logical data. The right side is used for more creative thinking, as well as emotional or relational thought. Obsessive-compulsives tend to rely primarily on the data-oriented part of their thinking. In fact, obsessives have a strong tendency to deny most emotional feelings or responses, even though they are frequently dominated by strong, underlying emotions. You might say that the obsessive *feels* with his mind.

Furthermore, obsessive-compulsives have a tendency to criticize themselves and others for being less than perfect. Coupled with that is a drive toward control—of self, circumstances, personal environment, and others. Many people tend to feel inferior at some time and try to compensate for those feelings of inferiority. For the obsessive-compulsive, those inferiority feelings lead to power struggles because of their strong motivation to be in control. Both internal and interpersonal conflicts often result.

The vice-president of a Fortune 500 company was strongly control-oriented. Throughout his division, he insisted on personally supervising and approving even the simplest decisions, such as which office supplies the secretaries purchased and from which vendors they ordered them. As a result, his area of responsibility was constantly under severe tension.

DIRT-OBSESSED

The obsessive-compulsive's concern with dirt gives us a candid look at perfectionism. The key question is, How clean is clean enough? As a young boy, one of the authors was taught by his mother how to wash dishes. He never enjoyed the chore, partly because he never knew how clean was clean enough, and partly because his mother was somewhat obsessive-compulsive herself. She always insisted that the dishes be carefully scrubbed in scalding water, rinsed in hot water to remove all germs, then rinsed again in cold water to remove all traces and residue of soap (which might have caused diarrhea). Finally, the dishes needed to be carefully dried and put away.

As he did the dishes, this individual often wrestled with the question, How hot does the water have to be and for how long must the dishes be immersed in it to kill every single germ? In fact, can that be done? Is it worth the trouble? What if one germ slips through? The result of this kind of obsession is obvious: childhood training that spawns such fearful thoughts can cause children to develop obsessive-compulsive personality problems later.

Dirt in other areas of life—personal hygiene, housekeeping, laundry—is often an obsession. "Cleanliness is next to godliness" is the maxim that spells disaster for some obsessive-compulsives. To them, perfect cleanliness can mean the next best thing to perfection itself. It becomes a substitute for washing one's imperfections away so that one can be more perfect and acceptable.

MONEY-FOCUSED

The obsessive-compulsive tends to be financially conservative, which can be a positive trait; however, this particular characteristic is often taken to the extreme. Because of a strong need to feel secure and in control, obsessives tend to be strongly money-oriented. In fact, many obsessive-compulsive corporate treasurers will treat funds as though they were their own, rather than the company's. They will not only exercise the conscientious stewardship demanded of a person serving in that position but will also treat any expenditure as a personal affront, justifying such an attitude in the name of financial conservatism.

At times, an obsessive-compulsive husband may deeply resent his wife's need to spend money on their children, a new hairdo, a dress, or on other personal expenses, all because of his strong desire to save that money for the future.

TEMPTATIONS OF THE O-C

Like every other person, the obsessive-compulsive has a nature that manifests itself in selfish behavior. With more than five billion people on planet Earth, each of us feels insignificant and inferior to some extent. We all try to compensate for those feelings through selfish or inappropriate behavior patterns. Three such behavior patterns are (1) materialism, or preoccupation with money and material things, (2) power struggles, a desire to control, dominate, or be more prominent than other people, and (3) sexual and other physical enticements.

Obsessives can fall into sexual temptation, especially because of their tendency to deny emotions, their own sexuality, or their need for emotional intimacy. However, they tend to be tempted primarily in two other areas—materialism and power struggles.

MATERIALISM

Because of their preoccupation with money, obsessives can become very materialistic. Frequently, their materialistic behaviors are hidden under the guise of "saving for the future." Sometimes obsessive-compulsives refuse to give to others because of their strong drive to build up personal security by saving. The possession of money is not wrong, but the *love* of money is the root of all kinds of evil. Although the love of money is obvious and overt in other personalities, it may be more subtle in the obsessive-compulsive and therefore more difficult to recognize or confront.

POWER STRUGGLES

A second major area of temptation, and perhaps the most crucial for obsessive-compulsives, is the desire for power, or what has been called the "pride of life." Because they themselves usually have experienced a great deal of conditional love, obsessive-compulsives tend to approach others with the same attitude. As one obsessive-compulsive put it, "I love my fellow workers unconditionally just as long as they measure up to my performance standards." That same person later acknowledged that such personal feelings were at the root of several intense on-the-job conflicts in his working environment.

The intensely competitive nature of obsessive-compulsives frequently makes them successful in their work. Yet the kind of success they achieve often leaves them relationally empty.

It is important for the obsessive-compulsive to work at avoiding inappropriate obsessive behavior patterns, especially crucial ones such as workaholism, materialism, power struggles, and self-critical, perfectionistic behavior. How to do that will be explored later.

AT THE END OF MY ROPE

Obsessive-compulsives tend to have a high number of idealistic expectations. An obsessive-compulsive expects an enthusiastic response to new programs, a willingness to become involved in work projects, and faithful attendance at committee and activity meetings. Closely related to idealism and unfulfilled expectations is bitterness, the most significant factor in burnout. As we discussed in earlier chapters, bitterness, which involves prolonging anger with a vengeance motive, is the result of holding grudges. It is an even greater factor in burnout than stress or perfectionistic personality traits.

When our idealistic expectations about marriage, work relationships, material gains, or other factors in life are not met, the natural result is for us to feel angry toward someone or something. We may be angry at our spouse for not being the "perfect marriage partner" (even though we ourselves are imperfect), or angry at our supervisor or fellow workers for failing to appreciate our efforts to improve the quality of work in the workplace.

Here are two statements commonly heard from people who suffer from burnout.

1. "Nobody sees or appreciates the adversity I am experiencing." The second is similar to it, but subtly different.

2. "Life isn't fair. I'm getting a raw deal."

When our idealism is shattered, we start to feel that life isn't fair, and we naturally look around for someone or something to blame. The anger produced by blame confronts us with a choice. We must either forgive, or by default we will choose to harbor anger and resentment, which ultimately leads to bitterness and easily infects those around us. Bitterness can affect marriage relationships, as well as other relationships.

MARITAL CONFLICT

In Frank Minirth's research on the obsessive-compulsive personality type, a number of characteristics are isolated that weaken the marriage relationship when they are present in the extreme. Even in courtship, the obsessive-compulsive tends to be characterized by caution or restraint. In some respects, this is a positive trait, preventing premarital sexual involvement or making a commitment to the wrong person. However, some obsessives can be so perfectionistic in their courtship that they never find the "perfect" mate.

Making a marriage commitment is extremely difficult for the perfectionist since he tends to live in the future a great deal of the time, working for a tomorrow that never arrives. A marriage commitment in the here and now can be a risky venture.

Once married, O-Cs have other problems. For example, Jerry, a successful businessman with many O-C traits, demanded that his wife, Julie, be totally loyal to him. In fact, he often became infuriated with her when she gave time to other people, demanding that she "fulfill her role" to meet his needs. Despite these demands on his wife, Jerry had trouble recognizing that he himself was far from totally committed to her. Instead, he was a workaholic who was committed to his job "110 percent." He often worked overtime and weekends, forgetting even to call his wife to let her know that he would not be home in time to enjoy the meal that he still expected her to prepare so carefully.

Jerry's attitude illustrates several other difficulties O-Cs encounter in their marriage relationships.

- *They give minimal commitment but demand maximal commitment.*

Obsessives seem to have a tendency to think of themselves as being more committed than they really are. They often give themselves credit for not being involved in sexual affairs, counting that restraint as true loyalty to their partners. They fail to see the disloyalty in their workaholism or in their unwillingness to share themselves, that is, to communicate their basic, inner feelings.

- *They limit intimacy.*

Obsessives have an intense fear of vulnerability or lack of control, which includes emotional vulnerability. To express feelings is to give up a measure of control and to admit weakness, something the obsessive dares not do.

- *They need to control both themselves and those around them.*

That need frequently results in power struggles within a marriage, especially if both spouses are strong O-Cs. In such cases, control can extend from such petty issues as whether the toothpaste tube is squeezed from the end or the middle to such major issues as vocation or the number of children desired.

- *They do only (what they consider to be) their share in the marriage.*

That leads to a kind of "50-50" marriage relationship, one that is less than ideal or successful. Our conviction is that a marriage can be successful only when both partners give 100 percent to the relationship. When one, or both partners, looks to do only his share, resentments and conflict will naturally build.

- *They experience unspontaneous and routine sexual function.*

Over a period of time, obsessives will have a tendency to ignore the physical dimension of communication in marriage, replacing sexual harmony and spontaneity and emotional and verbal communication with an increased commitment to work or to acquiring material things.

We have seen marriages in which both partners pursued their individual interests for years. Although they lived under the same roof, they were like ships passing in the night. The husband had his work, his golf, his fishing, and his interest in football; the wife had her tennis and her social club or church activities. In some marriages the only commonalities were the children and the problems. It's no wonder that such marriages die on the vine. Since obsessive-compulsives have a great capacity to work and to exhibit commitment, it's sad that they fear commitment in interpersonal relationships and therefore fail to work on the area that is such a high priority—marital harmony.

We encourage obsessives to give up perfectionism in marriage, to avoid bitterness, to work on sharing personal communication verbally, not just physically, and to learn to enjoy their partner as a best friend.

We have examined two consequences of O-C behavior: personal burnout and marital conflict. However, those consequences need not come to pass. In the next chapter, we will consider some ways to cure excessive obsessive-compulsive behavior.

9
FACING
MY FEELINGS

This chapter is being written while I am seated in a DC-9 aircraft on a Monday morning against the beautiful mountain backdrop of Colorado Springs. However, I shouldn't be here right now. This aircraft was scheduled to leave nearly two hours earlier than it did. First, we experienced a fog delay. A half hour later, while we were taxiing into position for takeoff, the pilot ran the aircraft off the edge of the runway. We were stuck in the mud for almost two hours. Finally, the plane was pulled from the mud, restored to the runway, and readied for takeoff. During the delay the pilot consoled us over the intercom, "I feel terrible about this. It is an awful way to begin a Monday morning. I know most of you have tight schedules and connecting flights to make."

How did the passengers feel? Most were fairly good-natured, but several voiced anger over fouled-up flight schedules and connections. Others were fearful of missing important meetings or appointments. And underlying several of the conversations with flight attendants were feelings of guilt for expressing those emotions of anger and fear. It was obvious that many of those passengers had a significant number of obsessive-compulsive traits.

Although most obsessive-compulsives have strong feelings, they do not like to feel. They would much rather think. They keep their emotions hidden from others and, if possible, from themselves. As a result, obsessive-compulsives may seem cold and indifferent.

Rick was known as a gifted communicator and a capable administrator. Yet many people considered him to be cold in his personal relationships, unfeeling, and unable to relate to the emotional expressions of others. Speaking to a member of our counseling staff,

Rick conceded that he was more interested in facts than in feelings. And even though as a minister he recognized the need for counseling and other people-oriented services, he strongly preferred to study in his office with the door closed while his secretary screened personal calls and visits.

EMOTIONS

What emotions do most obsessive-compulsives actually feel? Let's examine some typical O-C emotions and how they deal with them.

ANGER

According to a number of authorities, a primary emotion of obsessives is anger. Many obsessive-compulsives had strong, dominant parents who demanded unquestioning obedience and forbade their children to express anger, classifying such as tantamount to rebellion. Thus, in early life the obsessive-compulsive developed a struggle between obedience and defiance.

Outwardly, obsessives are usually extremely compliant, so we know that the pull of obedience usually wins. Occasionally, however, defiance wins. When obsessives submit or comply, that obedience frequently generates feelings of strong anger, sometimes even rage. As one obsessive-compulsive housewife put it, "Both my parents expected me always to do exactly what they said. I usually did, but underneath I seethed."

When asked, "Did you ever decide not to comply with their wishes?" her reply was, "Seldom. I was scared to death whenever I didn't do what they said."

FEAR

On the rare occasions when obsessives allow defiance to win out over their inclination toward obedience, the act of defiance will later lead to even stronger feelings of fear of authority. Actually that emotion is fear of parental authority left over from childhood.

Although obsessive-compulsives do not like to admit it, they are frequently dominated by powerful emotions of intense anger or fear. Their fears tend to lead to perfectionistic traits and to future compliance, whereas the feelings of anger or rage often lead to nonper-fectionistic traits and a present refusal to comply.

Thus, although obsessive-compulsives tend to be conscientious in most areas of their lives, they usually have a few areas in which they tend to be extremely negligent. For example, one obsessive-compulsive who was always punctual, orderly, and neat frequently misplaced his keys. An obsessive-compulsive housewife who managed two children, a husband's career, and a college-level computer course successfully, nonetheless found it extremely difficult to maintain any semblance of neatness in her home. Obsessive-compulsives often tend to be characterized by opposing traits that arise from their mixed feelings.

Just what does the obsessive-compulsive fear? He fears:

Dependency. He prefers relationships in which he is in control and others are dependent on him.

Close relationships. Close relationships demand emotional vulnerability or dependency, feelings that are unthinkable and highly undesirable to the obsessive-compulsive.

Loss of control. Being in control of himself and having control over his circumstances is of extreme importance to the O-C. He feels helpless and fears those feelings of helplessness whenever he loses control. The more he experiences feelings of powerlessness, the more an obsessive under stress wants to "do something about it," even when the appropriate course of action may be to be patient.

GUILT

Related to anger and fear are the feelings of guilt experienced by most obsessive-compulsives. Although guilt is a valid emotion to warn us when we are wrong, we tend to experience one of two extremes of this emotion. Self-centered, sociopathic personalities (aspects of which all of us are born with to some degree) tend to minimize or ignore feelings of guilt while persisting in selfish or sociopathic behavior that fulfills the description of having "consciences seared with a hot iron." They seldom feel guilty, even when they should.

On the other hand, some people, because of strict upbringing and exposure to legalistic teaching, feel guilty about almost anything. For example, one of the authors was raised in a strict home where reading a newspaper was not allowed on Sunday. It took years for him to feel comfortable when sitting down to scan the front page, the sports section, or even the comics, because of his inappropriate guilt.

Many obsessive-compulsives are plagued by an overly strict conscience, one that causes continued feelings of guilt and lack of self-forgiveness long after the failure has passed. For example, a conscientious college student was cheating in school primarily because of years of being unsuccessful and experiencing parental disapproval. When he was caught and confronted with his misconduct, he confessed to the school authorities. During the balance of his college career, he maintained a "clean slate." However, feelings of guilt and even depression over the incident continued to plague him years later, hampering his efforts to meet the needs of others. Like many of his obsessive-compulsive colleagues, the student had admitted his failure to live up to a standard of absolute perfection and had accepted forgiveness. Yet he could not forgive himself or quiet his hyperactive conscience.

Because of the tendency to deny feelings or to turn them inward, O-Cs tend to experience a greater degree of depression than almost any other personality type.

Another kind of obsessive-compulsive, however, has a tendency to hold in feelings of anger and then occasionally ventilate them, often in hostile, aggressive, or inappropriate ways. In fact, as one obsessive-compulsive businessman put it, "It is much easier for me to express myself when I am feeling angry with my wife than when I want to express warmth." Through intensive counseling he discovered the reason. It turned out that he was extremely fearful of becoming emotionally close or dependent and used anger to maintain what he considered to be a safe distance in his relationships.

Obsessive-compulsives become angry with others who affect or limit their ability to be "perfect" and with themselves for their own imperfections.

DEFENSE MECHANISMS

Frequently, the obsessive-compulsive copes with his feelings by using defense mechanisms. Defense mechanisms are the automatic, subconscious ways we respond to conflict or frustration. In essence, they are ways in which we deceive ourselves to avoid facing our true desires, emotions, and motives.

Although every individual practices defense mechanisms many times each day, certain defenses are most common to obsessive-compulsives. Let's examine these mechanisms.

DENIAL

An individual using this defense mechanism denies access to consciousness of thoughts, feelings, or motives. Although denial is most commonly seen in histrionic or hysteric (outwardly emotional, attention-seeking) personalities, obsessives frequently practice denial of emotions such as anger or fear. For example, one obsessive-compulsive professional was experiencing marital conflict, yet insisted that he had never been angry with his wife. What he meant was that he had never allowed himself to get in touch with his feelings of anger—feelings that in many instances were already evident to his wife.

INTELLECTUALIZATION

Individuals who intellectualize may develop strong inferiority feelings. Yet they cover those feelings by attempting to impress others, using extensive philosophical discussion, technical jargon, and intellectual vocabulary. We knew a graduate student who spent hours in the coffee shop discussing philosophical issues and debating obscure concepts. But in spite of all that discussion, he never got in touch with his feelings.

ISOLATION

The individual who practices isolation separates unacceptable feelings from his conscious awareness. This is one of the more common ways obsessives deal with anger, particularly those who have been taught that all anger is wrong. At times, individuals who believe feelings of greed or lust are totally unacceptable isolate those emotions in spite of the fact that most normal people do experience them from time to time.

REACTION FORMATION

Often linked with isolation, reaction formation involves adopting attitudes or actions that are the exact opposite of conscious or unconscious impulses. An example would be a television evangelist who preaches long sermons against materialism but secretly holds large bank accounts. Or a father who has strict and complex rules designed to forbid his teenagers from having any physical contact with the opposite sex, but who secretly reads pornographic magazines.

HYPOCRISY

Those who practice hypocrisy become increasingly self-righteous. The hypocrite thanks God that he is not like others—robbers, alcoholics, adulterers—and carefully maintains a list of dos and don'ts, tailor-made to his personal preferences but which is designed to maintain his own personal selfishness, hostility, and anger. Those who practice hypocrisy frequently regard anyone less legalistic than themselves as less good or even diabolical. They make a great show of religious ritual to cover up their inappropriate emotions.

MAGICAL THINKING

Magical thinking is a defense mechanism by which individuals compensate for feelings of inferiority by fooling themselves into thinking they have some supernatural powers. This tends to be present to a greater degree in obsessive-compulsive adults and young children than in other groups of people. It is extreme in those suffering from schizophrenia but manifests itself more mildly in obsessives.

Magical thinking frequently leads to guilt in obsessives who become angry at friends or relatives who later experience some tragedy. One young obsessive housewife had shouted over the telephone at her mother the day before her mother suffered an automobile accident. Her mother later died of the resulting injuries. It took months of intensive therapy to help that obsessive-compulsive individual recover from her magical thinking that left her believing that she had in some way caused the fatal mishap.

UNDOING

Undoing is the unhealthy side of appropriate restitution, that is, offering an apology or attempting to right specific wrongs we have done to others. Obsessives and others who practice undoing try to perform positive verbal communication or benevolent acts, attempting to counter other negative acts. The problem is, they do so without acknowledging the wrong deeds, as if they had never made the errors.

One example of undoing involved a lady who frequently criticized the members of her women's club behind their backs. However, when she was with them, she was warm, effusive, and outgoing in her praise and encouragement—almost to excess. Because she considered herself to be a highly encouraging and positive individual, she managed to use that undoing as a means of escaping personal awareness of her gossip and criticism. Whether with respect to inappropriate thinking or undesirable emotions, obsessive-compulsives often find it extremely painful to face the truth.

Though it may be painful to discover the truth about such emotions as guilt, fear, and anger, as well as about our dualistic and inappropriate thinking, it is important for us to progressively give up our defense mechanisms in order to become more emotionally and spiritually healthy.

PROJECTION

Almost everyone uses projection. For example, a person who has strong cravings for attention but is unaware of them will tend to condemn others. Likewise, the person who is in denial about anger toward another person will frequently accuse that person of "being angry at me," projecting his own anger onto the other individual.

RATIONALIZATION

Frequently engaged in by obsessive-compulsives, rationalization is a means of justifying unacceptable attitudes, beliefs, or behavior by the misapplication of logic or the invention of false reasons.

REPRESSION

The most general of all defense mechanisms and the foundation for denial, repression involves banishing unacceptable ideas, feelings, impulses, or motives from our conscious awareness.

DISPLACEMENT

Displacement involves transferring an emotion from its original object to a more acceptable substitute—such as "kicking the cat" when you're really angry at your spouse or boss.

SOMATIZATION

Somatization also involves transferring unacceptable emotions or feelings to the physical realm (for example, headaches, stomachaches, heartburn). Thus individuals are able to keep their minds on their physical symptoms in order to avoid becoming aware of their true emotions and motives.

SARCASM

Individuals with a repressed hostility toward themselves or even a group may ventilate that hostility without being aware of it by making critical jokes about themselves or others.

10
TYPE A
OBSESSIVE-COMPULSIVES

Many obsessive-compulsive workaholics are also Type A personalities. Type A personalities have distinct personality characteristics and a distinct way of thinking. They exhibit the following characteristics:

TYPE A BEHAVIOR PATTERNS

HIGH COMPETITIVENESS

Everything Type A's do becomes competition, even in relationships. That sometimes causes them to encourage competitiveness in their children. As a result, a Type A workaholic usually pushes his children to strive after achievements, rather than accepting them for who they are. Spouses compete with each other, sabotaging meaningful communication and peaceful coexistence in the home. Their competitiveness also affects their job circumstances and even their recreational activities.

EXCESSIVE STRIVING FOR ACHIEVEMENT

Involve a Type A obsessive-compulsive in conversation, and soon the subject becomes his or her latest project or list of achievements—either those he has already accomplished or those he is about to perform. He or she usually experiences an inability to say no. Thus, as time passes, the list of things to do generally grows longer rather than shorter.

IMPATIENCE OR HURRY SICKNESS

Type A obsessive-compulsives despise waiting for elevators. They would much rather take the stairs, even if there are twenty flights. They can't stand being placed on hold on the telephone, and traffic tie-ups sometimes leave them feeling physically ill. As one Type A person described it, "For me and others like me, life probably consists of three words: *hurry, worry,* and *bury*."

A consequence of this trait is that because of his schedule, the Type A workaholic generally finds it hard to spend more than a few minutes in passing with his children. Also, time spent with children is generally relational rather than task-oriented, so it is even more difficult for him to make the effort to be with them. Since Type A workaholics frequently can't say no to anyone, they usually end up saying no to their families by default. Such behavior patterns led to the writing of such books as *When I Relax I Feel Guilty*.

AROUSED ANGER AND HOSTILITY

When asked whether their fathers gave them more positive or negative verbal feedback and reinforcement, a group responded almost unanimously that they received 75 to 90 percent negative feedback. As one of them put it, "My dad was always blowing his stack at me. He came home with all this anger from work and took it out on us kids—especially me, since I was the oldest."

TYPE A THINKING

Obsessive-compulsive personalities usually have strong mental capacities and seem to be fact-oriented. They are ideal for jobs that demand an ability to master a number of facts. Good researchers, accountants, computer programmers, airline pilots, air traffic controllers, nurses, doctors, pastors, theologians, business administrators, managers, and many other professional workers are often balanced obsessive-compulsive individuals who utilize factual, organizational, and work-ethic strengths.

However, although obsessives are thinkers, they do not always think accurately. The following are a sampling of some irrational beliefs held by Type A obsessive-compulsives.

- *Quantity of output is more important than quality of output.*

The major emphasis of Type A obsessive-compulsives is to "churn out" a lot of work. For instance, three highly productive obsessive-compulsives decided to form a "book of the month" club. However, they weren't planning to read a book each month. They intended to *write* a book each month, on top of their already busy schedules and other demands.

Every day Joe makes lists of fifteen to twenty things to do. He feels motivated to check off his list daily, even if the items are poorly or sloppily done. It doesn't bother him if they're not done well, but it does bother him if they are not checked off. But excellence is not simply a matter of checking off items on a list. It involves establishing a balance between quality and quantity, even as we recognize that we are not perfect in either category. Instead, success means giving our best in any given situation.

- *Faster is always better.*

Many obsessives' lives are like a treadmill moving faster and faster. And somehow the charge of adrenaline from life in the fast lane motivates them to work even more rapidly. Though the passive-aggressive O-C tends to move slower and slower under pressure, the Type A obsessive works faster, talks faster, and even tries to think faster. Unfortunately, working faster doesn't always produce a better product. In fact, faster can create disaster.

Consider Wayne. Wayne works in a factory that rebuilds spark plugs. Although he was already doing a fine job reaching his assigned quota, he wanted to turn out more rebuilt spark plugs than the other workers. But in the process of working faster, he ruined an entire batch of plugs and cost the company a large sum of money. As a result, he was reprimanded for working *too* fast. Life is like freeway driving. We shouldn't be moving so fast or so slow that we're out of sync with the rest of the traffic.

- *Horrible disaster will occur if deadlines are not met.*

A highly successful radio professional became physically ill when, through a number of unavoidable circumstances, including equipment failure, a deadline was missed in the preparation of a documentary. Such feelings would have been perfectly understandable, except that in this case the deadline missed was seventy-two hours *before* the documentary was scheduled to be broadcast. In the October 19, 1976, *Family Health Magazine*, psychologist Leonard Cammer asks, "What about your punctuality? Mostly, it serves you in good stead, but can you allow yourself to be five or ten minutes late when it really would make no difference? Do you panic at the very thought?"

Here is one O-C who learned the benefits of waiting. Horace learned of a conflict in his office. His initial reaction was to attempt to gather all the people involved in the conflict in his office that day. Because of his schedule, however, he was unable to arrange the meeting. In the meantime, those directly involved in the problem got together and resolved it, probably much more adequately than if he had tried to wade into the conflict.

A lesson that many of us need to learn is that meeting deadlines is far less important than dealing with people, issues, or even taking time out. Paul Meier likes to give this advice to Type A obsessive-compulsives: Never do today what you can put off till tomorrow.

- *Winning or losing a competition is a reflection of my worth as a human being.*

In our society professional sports, business, and industry have produced a "win at all cost" mentality. Seminars are available to aid individuals in "winning" the game of life, which usually means successfully competing with others. College football fans from various universities discuss the relative merits of their teams and gauge which team will be crowned the national champion. In professional sports the Super Bowl, the World Series, and the NBA playoff finals settle the same question.

However, in any competition there is always one winner—and many losers. Unfortunately, we have somehow developed a connection that links personal worth to winning. Thus, when we lose, we feel horrible. A magazine article describes a twenty-game-winning major league pitcher as unable to accept losing and feeling totally worthless whenever it happened.

- *I am only as good as my accomplishments.*

This idea is closely linked with the previous belief. One way of spotting Type A obsessive-compulsive behavior, particularly the workaholic kind, is to check your conversation. Do you spend a lot of time talking about your accomplishments? (You may not be the best judge of this—so check with your wife or husband, your children, your business associates, or other professionals with whom you interact.) Frequently, we focus on our accomplishments because we feel we are *only as good as our achievements*. It is irrational to feel so competitive or achievement oriented that self-worth becomes linked to personal accomplishments. Nor will an endless string of achievements insure that we will like ourselves. Usually, a list of accomplishments simply produces either an appropriate response—being thankful—or an inappropriate response—feeling that I am really special because of what I achieve, or worthless because of my inability to achieve. These feelings lead to another irrational belief.

- *Nonachievement-oriented activities are a waste of time.*

Why do the spouses of Type A obsessive-compulsive workaholics frequently complain that they are ignored when it comes to personal conversation? Why do their children often feel conditionally loved or, worse, neglected? Why do Type A's look for excuses to work overtime, bring work home from the office, and try to do three or four things at once? Because of the irrational conviction that nonachievement-oriented activities are just a waste of time. Wasting time can certainly be classified as a sin, but it is probably not as great a sin as most Type A O-Cs assume. Furthermore, the list of activities considered time-wasters by Type A O-Cs is a lot longer than the lists other personality types would create. Although rest is an activity considered a time-waster by many Type A O-Cs, there is positive value to time away from the productive mind-set.

We should place a premium on certain nonachievement-oriented activities such as relationships, rest, and even waiting.

- *I can have complete control over my life if I only try hard enough.*

The obsessive-compulsive is often convinced, without rational foundation, that just a little more effort will give him or her complete control over circumstances, self, and even others. To the obsessive-compulsive, few things seem worse than "losing control." Obsessive-compulsives have been known to become extremely angry and depressed when placed in emotional circumstances that bring tears. In traffic, Type A obsessives sometimes believe they can make all the traffic lights if they just drive hard and fast enough. Being put on hold on the telephone, being caught in a traffic jam, spending time circling a busy airport—those kinds of uncontrollable situations make life miserable for the Type A obsessive-compulsive. A frequent corollary to this for the Type A is the thought that speeding up the pace of his activities is the best way to keep or regain control.

- *Being perfectionistic is the best way to insure high quality achievements.*

A successful, obsessive-compulsive medical doctor had always made straight A's throughout high school and college. When he reached medical school, suddenly he found himself to be just one of the average students, since all the rest of the medical students were also the "cream of the crop" in their high schools and colleges. To assure himself of quality achievements, this doctor became increasingly perfectionistic and, in the process, became highly critical of himself and others. His marriage relationship became strained, and his friends began to avoid him. He expected perfection of himself and of others. He had not reconciled himself to the fact that nobody is perfect.

Often, relaxing perfectionistic standards lead to greater excellence and more successful results than perfectionism does. On one of our radio programs former major league catcher Jim Sundberg told of pushing himself and trying harder but being less successful at bat. But his average improved dramatically after his batting coach encouraged him to relax and have fun at the plate.

Being perfectionistic only underscores how far we can fall. We all fall short of perfection, which leads to feelings of anger and depression in the Type A obsessive.

- *Openly expressing my anger and hostility makes other people pay for getting in my way.*

Although many Type A obsessives would not admit to such thoughts, they tend to couch them in terms of "appropriate" confrontation. "I believe in taking a strong stand for my convictions." "I believe in confronting people when they need to be confronted." But the proper alternative to expressing anger is to acknowledge and confront it.

What we discover as we consider this facet of the Type A obsessive-compulsive is that, although he generally has superior thinking capabilities, he is susceptible to numerous irrational thoughts. Those thoughts are related to some very strong underlying emotions, ones the obsessive-compulsive refuses to acknowledge but which nonetheless play a key role in his or her life.

11
PERFECTIONISTS

Is it excellence or is it perfectionism?"

Our driven society today has a difficult time telling the difference between the two. In their nationwide best-seller *In Search of Excellence,* Thomas Peters and Robert Waterman isolate eight attributes that characterize excellent, innovative companies. The first two are (1) a bias for action, and (2) a people orientation, particularly toward the customers.[1] Our problem is that we sometimes have difficulty being able to tell the difference between excellence and a major modern distortion—perfectionism. We all should take pleasure in an appropriate, balanced attempt to meet high standards. There should be a legitimate concern for quality and order in our work. But this concern needs a balance. In fact, the eight traits shared by most of the companies Peters and Waterman considered excellent indicate a remarkable balance. For example, trait number 8 is defined as "simultaneous loose-tight properties." Furthermore, these successful companies encourage autonomy and entrepreneurship, yet stick closely to central core values of loyalty and commitment.

Perfectionism, on the other hand, is the fear-driven aim or obsession toward unrealistically high standards. Such a drive is frequently accompanied by intense anger toward self, others, and circumstances. The anger serves as a cover for an underlying fear that must be denied at all costs. The perfectionist is intensely hard on himself and extremely hard on others.

What are the major characteristics of a perfectionist?

HE CANNOT ACCEPT BEING LESS THAN PERFECT

This involves more than "a mild irritation." For example, during his early collegiate days, Chris Thurman was an extremely skilled tennis player; however, he frequently came close to giving up tennis altogether, particularly when on occasion he simply could not make every shot in a manner consistent with Bjorn Borg, the current top-ranked tennis player in the world.

HE BELIEVES HE IS WHAT HE DOES

His personal self-esteem is wrapped up in performance and achievement. Examples of this are almost too numerous to cite. Karrie, a nineteen-year-old college student, slim and attractive, is of average intelligence and able to grasp material. Yet she is devastated because her performance is not absolutely perfect. Part of Karrie's problem: her older brother Brady carried a 4.0 average through college. Karrie has already received two B's in her short career, thus dooming her, in her own opinion, to failure.

Justin, a computer programmer, cannot completely debug an innovative new program that he has written to solve the operational problems of the company for which he works. Although he has done a quality job, working well beyond the years of training he has and has been acknowledged as such by the man to whom he answers at work, Justin considers himself a failure. He simply hasn't performed, and he feels like a total flop.

HE BUYS INTO DISTORTED THINKING

This characteristic is closely related to the one above. Perfectionists are perhaps more susceptible to false beliefs than anyone else. For example, the perfectionist generally personalizes failure even though there may have been contributing factors. The perfectionistic husband chooses to ignore those and considers himself an absolute failure if he can't successfully complete a simple plumbing job, such as replacing leaky faucet washers. Never mind the fact that, as the CEO of a communications company, his daily skills and activities involve the use of words rather than plumbing tools. Never mind the fact that his skills allow him to earn ample funds to employ a plumber to take care of this task. He still feels like a failure, simply because he couldn't complete the plumbing task.

The perfectionist also catastrophizes anything less than perfection. Barbara, a career-minded young executive, determined to maintain the "perfect figure," especially since her mother tended toward being overweight. Barbara had a particular weakness for chocolate chip cookies. Generally, her self-discipline kept her from eating more than two or three at a time. And as she once confided in a friend, "I believe any time I've eaten one chocolate chip cookie, it's a disaster; two or more constitutes a catastrophe of epic proportions. I just know there's going to come a day when I've eaten one or two chocolate chip cookies and I'll just not be able to quit. And I'll be bigger than my mom. And no one will like me anymore."

This remarkably candid disclosure on the part of Barbara shows the harmful chain of thought processes so common to perfectionists. Furthermore, perfectionists take black and white thinking to extremes. One perfectionistic mother of a two year old tearfully unloaded on her mom, "I think I'm guilty of child abuse. I actually raised my voice at my two year old—and I was beginning to be upset with her." Although we recognize the dangers of parental abuse of young children, it is hardly abusive to acknowledge feelings of anger toward a child whose behavior patterns fit the classic "terrible twos." In fact, it's normal for such moms to lose patience at times.

Another example of such thinking was Bill, a twenty-eight year old who was raised in a strict religious family where weekly church attendance was a "nonnegotiable." Bill's position as a foreman in a large manufacturing plant involves a significant amount of shift work. Although he's good at his job and has learned to adjust to the schedule, he still feels horrible guilt pangs—even though he faithfully attends worship with his family whenever he's not working.

HE IS AFRAID OF PERSONAL DISCLOSURE

The perfectionist is absolutely frightened of personal disclosure —but his denial won't even let him admit he's afraid. For the perfectionist, the risk of anyone—even those who are close—knowing his real fears and weaknesses is simply beyond facing. The commercial for a well-known brand of deodorant, which featured the line "Never let them see you sweat," capitalized on this particular perfectionistic trait. Marketing their product to perfectionists in such a "felt need" way led to a substantial increase in market share.

The most common phrase used by perfectionists, though almost always unconsciously, is the phrase "Don't worry about it." Most perfectionists don't give a second thought before using this phrase; however, its use is loaded with meaning. What the perfectionist is really saying is, "Let's make it a point not to look at our feelings. Let's take action. Let's practice denial. Whatever it takes, the last thing we want to do is admit we're worried, or worse yet, fearful."

Some time ago one of the authors spoke to a large conference of professionals. They represented many backgrounds and a great deal of training—and most were perfectionistic. The topic was overcoming perfectionism and workaholism. At the close of the first day of the conference during a question-and-answer session, the speaker noted a significant amount of hostility on the part of the listeners. One particularly irate participant seemed to sum up the feelings of many of his colleagues, "Why are you trying to tell us this sort of thing? Don't you understand the importance of dedication? Of commitment? We've given our lives to serve others. Instead of telling us that we need to slow down, you need to be telling our constituents to get with the program." Another added, "Don't you understand that our jobs demand 100 percent commitment? We're on duty twenty-four hours a day."

It took another twenty-four hours of speaking and interaction before any of the group finally began to acknowledge that there was a legitimate difference between excellence and perfectionism.

ENVIRONMENTS THAT LEAD TO PERFECTIONISM

Although some people may inherit the predisposition toward a perfectionistic personality, most of the perfectionism we have observed in those we counsel has come from the environment at home. Several particular traits stand out.

CRITICAL, HARD-TO-PLEASE PARENTS

Many perfectionists were raised by critical, hard-to-please parents. And we're not talking about healthy discipline or expectations, or about setting limits. We're talking about the parents who constantly voice put-downs or engage in fault finding. They seem to get a charge out of criticizing their kids. A good rule of thumb: 80 to 90 percent of a parent's communication ought to be positive—"catching" the son or daughter doing good—with the balance of a corrective nature. All too frequently parents who were themselves the object of parental criticism learn that style of parenting all too well. No matter what their children do, they aren't pleased.

Michael, for example, was the oldest son of a father who had excelled both academically and in sports. In high school Michael made mostly A's but occasional B's. On one particular report card he brought home 5 A's and an A-. Unfortunately Michael wasn't surprised by the one thing his dad noticed—and discussed in great detail—the minus attached to his A in physics. Never mind the difficulty of physics class or the fact that Michael had achieved A's in other difficult subjects. And never mind the fact that he was a member of the football team. He wasn't a starter and probably stood little or no chance of ever making all-district. Even though his dad hadn't been all-district, he had started for three years. Michael was subject to a father who was critical to the point of being impossible to please.

OVERINDULGENT PARENTS

Another cause of perfectionism in children, ironically, is the overindulgent parent. Strangely, this style of parenting frequently leads to the same result as the hard-to-please parent. Perfectionistic thinking grows out of a sense of "entitlement" fostered on the child by the parent. "You deserve the best." "You're the greatest." Though the child suspects that isn't really the case, the reinforcement of the overindulgent parent leads to unreasonable expectations and perfectionism.

AN UNSTABLE HOME SITUATION

Perhaps one of the most recognizable causes of perfectionism is an unstable home situation. It is not a coincidence that, in a day when one out of two marriages ends in divorce and when many homes are wracked by the effects of alcohol or drug abuse or other serious addictive behaviors, we are producing a generation of obsessive-compulsive perfectionists. Perhaps the one factor that can help simplify our understanding of what is essentially a complex situation is the concept of control.

When Dad and Mom divorce, or when Dad experiences frequent bouts of drunkenness, or Mom is addicted to rage, a child grows up with a rather accurate perception that things are out of control. The natural response is to seek to maintain and establish control at all costs.

Bryan Robinson, author of *Work Addiction* and professor of child and family development at the University of North Carolina at Charlotte, describes his own response to living in a chaotic family: "On my own, the need to control everything and everyone around me became an obsession. Things had to be done my way or not at all. But the old survival skills that saved me as a child no longer worked as an adult, causing me many problems in my interpersonal relationships at work, at home and at play."[2]

Bryan tells the story of one of his clients, Denton, a forty-year-old school administrator who grew up with an alcoholic mother. Denton had two jobs and spent the majority of his waking hours taking care of the responsibilities and duties of both jobs. From his own perspective Denton noted, "I know I can do things better, faster and more efficiently than most people can. . . . Even in elementary school, when the teacher would give an assignment, I would do more than what was required. If a report was to be five pages long, I'd do ten. If the teacher wanted me to help with the erasers, I'd straighten the desks, do a bulletin board, help correct papers and stack textbooks too. . . . I was doing what was right. I had to be the most outstanding one who did any task assigned to me. . . . As an only child, I could never predict what was going to happen. Because my father drank heavily on weekends, and my mother drank all the time, I felt the need to overcompensate. I didn't want my life turning out as unpredictable and chaotic and lacking in direction and goals as theirs."

The obsession with control evidenced by Denton isn't rare at all. It's the rule of perfectionists. It's one way they compensate for their unstable home situation.

Susan suffered from intense headaches—she lived on Extra Strength Tylenol.® She frequently yelled at her kids, snapped at her husband, constantly felt critical of herself. When she was a child, Susan's mother communicated to her, "We love you as long as you clean your plate, keep your room clean, take care of your pets, and don't do anything to embarrass us." At times she would say, "If you want Mommy to keep loving you, you'd better not talk back." On the wall in Susan's room hung a picture of Jesus. Frequently Susan's mother and dad would use the picture as a club to enforce good behavior. "He's watching you," they would say. "He won't like it if you misbehave. If you want Him to love you, you'd better be good. Don't forget—He's watching." It's no wonder with that kind of conditional love Susan became proficient at being perfectionistic.

RECOVERY COMES THROUGH WAITING

Perfectionism can be overcome, and in a later chapter, "Reaching Balance or Burnout" (chap. 14), we will discuss a number of specific steps you can take to reduce perfectionism in your life. But for now it's useful to remember that redirecting our attention toward what God has done for us can rekindle hope and help alleviate the symptoms of burnout.

Renewal of strength and hope is experienced by those who wait. One of the primary irritations confronting us in our fast-paced society is waiting. We wait for elevators and traffic lights, wait on delayed flights, stand and wait at the checkout counter of grocery stores, sit and wait in reception rooms of doctors' and dentists' offices, and otherwise occupy a great deal of time just waiting. Few of us enjoy it. Many of us become extremely impatient and irritated when forced to wait.

Waiting is an important ingredient, however, in our personal growth and development. It is designed to build into our lives a number of important traits, such as patience, perseverance, and self-control. One ancient word used for *wait* comes from a term describing a rope stretched taut. The waiting process is often a stretching one, one that is extremely difficult, but one that ultimately has a good end. And the significance of the term to today's burnout victim is important. Like an old and battered car, the burnout victim's strength is depleted. He has been many miles and feels he cannot long continue on. Yet he waits for renewed energy, purpose, and strength.

The picture of individuals who were faint, powerless, weary, and experiencing complete disaster, now soaring as eagles, running long distances without growing weary and walking without fainting describes an ancient principle that, when applied today, provides a workable cure for the spiritual dimension of burnout—renewed trust and hope.

One of the most common characteristics of advanced burnout is the loss of hope. Over recent years we have heard hundreds of individuals, housewives, students, lawyers, businessmen, accountants, executives, and others express the same thing: "I don't believe there's any hope of changing the situation."

Hope is an ingredient essential to withstanding the difficulties and pressures of life. It is an "anchor for the soul." We have seen severe emotional traumas and disorders overcome, seemingly irreparable marital conflicts healed and homes restored, and one tragedy after another endured—but only when there is hope.

A Midwestern businessman recently told us of several tragedies that had marked him and his wife. First, his son was killed in a traffic accident. Soon thereafter a daughter took her life on Christmas Day. Within a matter of months, another son took his life. How could he and his wife survive? Certainly, they had grieved over their losses, but as the man expressed it, "We didn't lose hope. We believe our children have trusted Christ as their Savior. Even though tragedy took them from us, we will see them again."

Don't despair. There is hope! There is a solution available. By turning attention away from self and one's seemingly hopeless, helpless condition and onto the everlasting God, the burnout victim can find strength renewed.

NOTES

1. Thomas Peters and Robert Waterman, *In Search of Excellence* (New York: Harper & Row, 1982), pp. 13-14.
2. Bryan Robinson, *Work Addiction* (Deerfield Beach, Fla.: Health Communication), p. 16.

12
DIFFERENT PERSONALITY TYPES AND STRESS

After sitting in on a radio program in which a panel of counselors discussed the obsessive-compulsive personality, a college administrator turned to a friend on the panel and said, "I don't like being an obsessive-compulsive, or whatever it is." Replied his friend, "I'm probably obsessive-obnoxious, and I'm not sure I like it either." During that call-in program, several people had phoned in to voice their dissatisfaction with the obsessive-compulsive personality traits in their lives.

Those individuals were missing an important point. Although we may not like certain aspects of our personalities, it is important that we come to accept ourselves. After all, we grow up in families where we developed the particular collection of personality strengths and weaknesses we have.

It is important to remember that each of us is unique, an unduplicated collection of traits and characteristics. We need to think of ourselves not with selfish pride or false humility but with sober judgment. We were each made for a purpose, one that is neither more nor less important than the purpose for other individuals.

HOW VARIOUS PERSONALITY TYPES ARE SUSCEPTIBLE TO BURNOUT

Most of us are fascinated with labels. In fact, we use labels in a variety of ways in the world in which we live. One of our greatest fascinations is with labeling people or personality types.

There is a wide range of ways in which people label personality differences. One of the earliest, developed by the Greek physician

Galen, involved four temperament types: sanguine, phlegmatic, choleric, and melancholic. Those temperament types provide the basis for a number of modern treatments of personality.

Another common personality characterization is called the DiSC —the dominant, influential, steady, and compliant. Developed by psychologist William Marston and refined by two other scholars, John G. Geier and Dorothy E. Downey, who developed the *Library of Classical Profile Patterns* and the *Personal Profile System,* the DiSC consulting instrument also involved numerous subcategories.[1]

For many years psychiatric literature has recognized some twelve or thirteen personality disorders. In their milder forms, some of those disorders have come to be recognized as personality traits or types.

Those traits include the *obsessive-compulsive* personality type, generally recognized as conscientious, dutiful, responsible, yet frequently perfectionistic. This kind of person tends to think about things over and over, likes to make lists, and focuses on performance.

The *hysteric* personality also focuses on performance, but more on performing for recognition than performing for success. Such individuals are frequently likable, outgoing, feeling-oriented, fun, and even dramatic. Often excitable, they can be emotionally unstable.

A third common personality type, the *passive-aggressive,* usually appears to be meek and dependent but often has strong emotions he works to keep buried. Passive-aggressives are commonly more dependent on others and may seem helpless or clinging. They have difficulty making decisions and are sometimes careless in their work. They may pout or procrastinate. They are often viewed as stubborn or uncooperative, and that assessment is usually accurate.

Another personality type is the *paranoid.* Such individuals tend to be hypersensitive, rigid, suspicious, or jealous. The paranoid personality is typically pessimistic. Paranoids expect the worst and often are hypersensitive toward others. Individuals with a high level of paranoid personality traits often have a great deal of trouble forgiving others. They commonly can recall in vivid detail the slightest offense from years past. Paranoids have a great deal of trouble trusting others, and they sometimes think they can read others' minds. They are quite sensitive and are very intuitive and able to sense another individual's motives.

Although there are other personality types we could consider, for purposes of this discussion we will catalog only one other: the *sociopathic,* or antisocial, personality. Although all of us have some antisocial traits, there are individuals who are intensely selfish, irresponsible, and impulsive and who live for the pleasure of the moment. The major characteristic of the sociopathic personality is an impaired superego, or conscience. Such an individual can engage in a wide range of activities without feeling guilt. Sociopathic individuals are users—and their use, or even abuse—of others leads to interpersonal conflicts. Quick to blame circumstances or those around them, they appear to be quite selfish—and generally they are.

THE OBSESSIVE-COMPULSIVE AND BURNOUT

The obsessive-compulsive personality is likely to keep performing right up to the moment he "crashes and burns." Since he is driven by internal factors and motivated by responsibilities, his approach to life is to push to the limit—and beyond. The internal voices of critical parents, the conditional acceptance he experienced in childhood, and his underlying attempt to gain control of himself and his circumstances often causes burnout—and sometimes causes him to inflict burnout on others. Obsessive-compulsives are driven and frequently drive those around them as well. They neglect rest and relationships. The O-C will often experience a mid-life crisis—and it seems that O-Cs are having mid-life-crises earlier these days than ever before—not a healthy sign in our driven society. The problem is that many in our society applaud the addiction to work that characterizes many O-Cs and that pushes them toward burnout.

The obsessive-compulsive, as we have seen, is most burnout prone. This personality overlaps with perfectionism and workaholism, as well as Type A behavior. Conscientious and dutiful, this individual tends to harbor—and to deny—anger while pushing himself to the limit.

Although the solution for burnout for obsessive-compulsives is complex, certain basic principles are helpful. Obsessives must learn to relax, to take time off from responsibilities, and to have fun. They need accountability for their addiction to work and someone to challenge them regarding an increasingly demanding schedule. They need to begin putting relationships before projects. And they need to learn to deal with underlying emotions, such as anger, guilt, or fear.

THE HYSTERIC PERSONALITY AND BURNOUT

The hysteric personality tends to be jovial and easygoing; however, the hysteric has a strong commitment to performance. These individuals feel as if they are always on stage. If they're not performing up to the standards of others and winning their approval, they frequently expend great quantities of emotional energy and burn out. They also may be susceptible to bitterness toward those who do not respond to their attempts to win friendship and approval.

If obsessives are likely to crash and burn, hysterics often respond to stress and burnout with a spectacular disaster. They will go down in dramatic fashion after using defense mechanisms such as denial, in which they refuse to acknowledge underlying emotions, or somatization, which involves transferring emotional thoughts into physical problems such as headaches or digestive tract disorders. Hysterics begin to experience increasing stress, eventually reaching a breaking point. That point may involve an extramarital affair or a sexual scandal, since hysterics seem to focus on sexual issues. Leonard was a prominent clergyman frequently seen on religious television programs. He came to one of our counselors for help after a public incident involving a prostitute. In therapy, Leonard admitted that he felt intensely burned out.

It turned out that in his childhood Leonard had been pampered and spoiled. His parents had praised him for his appearance. Furthermore, he had a great deal of anger toward the opposite sex as a result of conflicts with his mother, who alternated between critically denying him any privileges and lavishing attention on him.

Often hysterics under stress and facing burnout will "adopt" a prominent or popular diagnosis. We have seen this occur with a variety of diagnoses ranging from hypoglycemia to multiple personality disorder. The more dramatic the diagnosis the better. The point is, the hysteric is afforded some relief from the pressures that led to burnout and, in the process, gains attention.

Help for the hysteric is, again, not a simple matter. But there are certain principles that can aid him in overcoming stress and burnout. Usually a matter-of-fact approach is more helpful than expressing feelings of intense sympathy. Such a matter-of-fact approach can also tend to lessen the "drama" on which many hysterics thrive. Furthermore, it's important for hysterics to learn to think before they act. Directing their attention to analyzing behavior and considering its consequences can be very productive. Ultimately, hysterics need to be encouraged to take responsibility and to gain insight into the underlying emotional issues that frequently lead to burnout.

THE PASSIVE-AGGRESSIVE

Where obsessives crash and burn, and hysterics experience spectacular disasters, passive-aggressives often simply give up. They quit their jobs when facing stress and burnout. Or if they don't quit, they may write and act out a "failure script"—in other words, an unconsciously planned failure. Since they are given to obstruction, sabotage, pouting, and manipulation, they may use those particular techniques in bringing about their firing from a job or the breakup of a marriage.

Wally, a successful industrial worker for many years, found himself working approximately sixty to seventy hours a week. Renegotiation of his union contract brought about a reduction in wages, plus additional responsibility. Facing financial struggles, Wally grew careless on the job—and suffered a serious injury. He also began talking to a lawyer about filing for bankruptcy. Although he sought counsel from friends, he refused to accept their counsel—or kept coming up with reasons "those suggestions just wouldn't work."

This kind of individual tends to experience a great deal of anger but primarily internalizes it. He tends to ignore responsibility, to be late, yet do anything to avoid open conflict. The passive-aggressive personality burns out because of bitterness. He seems to be a nice, easygoing person—but he's often emotionally exhausted from "gunny sacking," or sticking large quantities of real or imagined hurts and insults into the emotional bag that he carries with him at all times.

Since passive-aggressives have been overprotected in childhood and left dependent, it's important to help them develop self-initiated strategies for resolving the crises of stress and burnout in their lives. Anything that can sharpen their decision-making skills is helpful. It's particularly crucial not to simply tell them what to do but to aid them in figuring out what their options are and which option to adopt. Finally, helping them face underlying emotions is of crucial importance.

THE PARANOID

The paranoid individual tends to be extremely sensitive. Usually deeply hurt in the past, he is especially attuned to every nuance of other people's communication. He is often suspicious, mistrustful, even envious. It's easy to go from paranoia to anger and bitterness.

Frequently paranoid personalities will adopt a "kill or be killed" approach. When under intense stress their attitude may be, "Shoot first, ask questions later." Their motto: "Do unto others before they do unto you." Usually the paranoid experiences burnout in some form of interpersonal conflict: a divorce, a major conflict at work, or a significant family quarrel.

Since paranoid personality early traits are frequently formed through deep hurts, including abuse in childhood or when they were relatively young, paranoid people are much like animals who have been caught in a trap and who are still experiencing the pain of being trapped.

Edwin was a middle-level manager who wasn't even aware of the intense pain he carried from conflicts with his father. Edwin professed deep allegiance to his boss, whom he admired a great deal and who had mentored him as well as recommended him for his position. Outwardly Edwin would do anything to show his loyalty to his boss.

One day, shortly after the company had reached a higher peak in sales than ever before, Edwin approached the top management of his company. He had three major criticisms of his boss—criticisms that would either cause his mentor to be fired or force him to resign.

Even though all those in management agreed that Edwin's evaluation was wrong, he insisted he was right. Ultimately, he lost his job and suffered greatly in his career.

Under stress the paranoid personality has great difficulty relating. Attack and retaliation are usually the options of choice. Thus it is important in trying to help paranoids through stress and burnout to be prepared to have them turn on you. It is crucial to be able to weather their storms, to be objective, and to maintain long-term loyalty until the paranoid is able to think more objectively.

Encouraging paranoids toward counseling to resolve underlying emotional pain is absolutely crucial. The cycle of pain, conflict, and crisis must be broken.

THE SOCIOPATH

Closely related to the narcissistic personality, this individual has an impaired conscience. His burnout usually comes from the consequences of self-indulgent behavior—sexual dissipation, drug or alcohol abuse, and so on. He may harbor bitterness but is more likely to ventilate his anger toward others—his tolerance of frustration is extremely low. Burnout in the sociopath is often related to the stresses he has brought upon himself.

Strangely, the sociopath tends to be the least likely to feel stressed out or burned out. The typical sociopathic attitude under stress could be summed up in the phrase "Take the money and run." Sociopaths have usually been coddled or spoiled in childhood. Frequently they have developed strong feelings of entitlement. The superego, or conscience, has been limited in development, and in most instances the loss of a significant love object, perhaps a parent, has occurred—a loss for which there has been no emotional resolution.

Because of the sociopath's tendency to use and blame others, in the absence of feelings of guilt the sociopath will frequently wind up in interpersonal conflicts—like the paranoid—but for different reasons. Paranoids and obsessives will tend to feel guilt over those conflicts. The sociopath always thinks, "It's the other guy's fault—it isn't me." Subconsciously his attitude is that people, jobs, and other aspects of his life exist for his own enjoyment.

David, a charismatic public speaker, rose from a minor political office to become a state senator. Caught in the aftermath of a real estate scandal and implicated and indicted, his approach was to blame everyone else. At first he tried literally to take a supply of funds he had amassed and run—in other words, leave the country. Ultimately brought to trial, he continued to insist that he was not at fault.

Finally, in therapy, he began to gain insight into the impairment of his conscience and to his own lack of responsibility. Today, after serving a short prison sentence (he was released early because of good behavior), David is working to help others who have run afoul of the law.

It's particularly important when trying to help the sociopathic person, especially with his narcissistic tendencies, to avoid being conned. Often a matter-of-fact confrontation—perhaps even an intervention involving a number of significant people in the individual's life—has to take place before the person will finally come to change his or her thinking, deal with issues that need to be resolved, and take a more responsible attitude toward life.

NOTE

1. John G. Geier and Dorothy E. Downey, *Library of Classical Profile Patterns* (Minneapolis: Performax Systems International, 1979); *Personal Profile System* (Minneapolis: Performax Systems International, 1977); both works now held by Carlson Learning Company, Minneapolis.

13
A WHOLISTIC REMEDY
FOR BURNOUT

Unfortunately, the corporate world today often makes a virtue of "facts only" thinking. Most graduate business programs teach the student to use the "scientific method" alone in solving business problems, using only facts and logic. That means the emotional side of the employee, as well as of the supervisor, is totally ignored. We agree with a well-known executive management consultant's assessment that if a business would deal with the emotional side of an employee, the whole person, it would have a much more productive worker.

In his consulting business, the same man deals with how clients and their employees are feeling. He says that too often business and industry take great employees and continually push them to increased productivity levels until they burn out and start producing less and less. When that happens, industry's "solution" is simply to fire them and hire replacements. However, statistics show that it takes about two years to get a new employee to the point of productivity of an established worker. He recommends that, instead of firing employees who are not producing well, it is more productive to find a niche for them that is better suited to their personality strengths. That means paying attention to the way employees feel about and relate to the world around them. That policy is followed by Japanese businesses, which today have far higher productivity averages than American businesses.

CARING FOR THE WHOLE WORKER

Another policy followed in Japan is that employee exercise periods and other breaks are adhered to strictly. Psychiatric studies have proved that such work styles are superior to those generally followed in American business, where employees are much more susceptible to burnout.

An example from one consultant's own experience, one with an ironic twist, validates that thinking. This consultant was working for a Fortune 500 company, where all the other junior executives came early, stayed late, and always carried home briefcases filled with papers to work on at night. He, however, worked only regular hours and, although he took home a briefcase every night to show everyone that he wasn't shirking, there was never anything in it!

He had already realized that competing with others to become an officer of the company wasn't a worthy goal. As he is fond of saying, "The only things you're going to be able to take into eternity with you are your spouse and children."

As a result, he concentrated on his family and his health outside of regular office hours. He then showed up every morning at work feeling rested and ready to put his all into his job during the regular work day. He laughs when he observes that he was then given one of the first promotions among his "class" of junior executives, with a bonus of an extra week's vacation. Why? Because his superiors were sure that he was spending too much overtime on his work in order to accomplish as much as he did!

When workers are young, it is easy for them to work hard, fast, and long, without taking time to pause and reflect on what they are doing. They hope that such a work pace will get them the prestige and prosperity they want in their career within a certain number of years, at which time they plan to be able to sit back, relax, and enjoy life and their families. Meanwhile, their health deteriorates and their families desert them, either physically or emotionally, since families can't wait all those years for satisfactory relationships. In his later years, the president of a large, successful construction company in the Midwest often said, "Slow down and take time to think. I wish I had done that when I was young, instead of working fifteen to twenty hours a day."

Another company president, George, spoken of previously, also learned the value of slowing down and accomplishing more. When he received psychiatric help at our clinic, he came to realize that at age fifty there were certain things he should not be able to do as well and as rapidly as he could at thirty, but there were other things that he should be able to do better. He had new physical limitations, but he was now a lot wiser than he was at thirty. At fifty he should be using his wisdom and experience to bring success to his company rather than his "elbow grease."

So George cut back to a thirty-five-hour work week and began accomplishing a significant amount of good through wise decision making and learning to delegate more to people under him. In fact, his company did better after he slowed down to thirty-five hours a week than it had done when he was working sixty hours a week every week—and so did his family.

That proves another point counter to the thinking of most workaholics and burnout victims. No one is indispensable. There are other people who can do the jobs or at least part of the jobs as well, if not better, than they can. That doesn't mean the burnout victim isn't needed. It means only that he or she can be more successful in a concentrated area while using much less energy than if he burns out.

As Howard Hendricks says, "When you play the game of climbing the ladder to success, you may reach the top only to find that the ladder was resting against the wrong wall."[1] Family members who take the time to enjoy one another and the simpler things in life, even if they have to sacrifice materialistic niceties to do so, are almost always happier than those who are bringing in more money but have to sacrifice time with one another.

Of course, there are times when career transitions may make it necessary to work harder or longer for several months. But even then a time limit should be set on how long one will continue to keep up such a pace and ignore or give lesser attention to other important areas of life.

TAKING CARE OF YOURSELF

Escaping or reversing burnout primarily involves taking care of yourself physically, mentally, and spiritually, and allowing others to help you in that task. But, first of all, you have to decide to take the initiative yourself, realizing that taking care of self is our responsibility. Without meeting that responsibility, we will never be able to succeed in our lifelong purposes.

At our clinic, we often have patients complete a "Taking Care of Yourself" test, which gives them and us some idea of how well they are accomplishing that task. We have divided the test questions into two categories: the physical and emotional/spiritual, even though some of the questions include elements of both categories.

The following are the questions to the physical part of this questionnaire and the advice we give our patients, including those suffering from burnout. Except in cases of suicidal thinking (discussed in the next chapter), we advocate making changes in the physical areas of a burnout victim's life first. Just feeling better physically often begins to change a person's burned out emotions and gives him or her the strength to begin other changes.

PHYSICAL CARE

- *Did you exercise three times this past week?*

The medical profession has maintained for years that being in good physical condition makes a noticeable difference in longevity and good health. Exercise can help keep off excess weight, control blood pressure, keep the heart healthy, and even ward off other diseases.

We have long recognized that people become addicted to negative things, such as drugs and alcohol. However, we now know that they can become addicted to positive things also. William Glasser showed that people can become addicted to jogging. Such an addiction has a physical reason. Certain chemicals, released from the body during jogging and other healthful exercise, cause a sense of well-being.

- *Did you eat a balanced diet this week?*

Diet is a major factor in the realm of physical health. Most nutritionists agree that the best diet is a balanced one that includes a little of all the food groups—meat and other proteins, vegetables, fruit, dairy products, and bread, cereals, and other grain products.

If you need to be on a weight-reducing diet, make sure it includes all the food groups, but less of each. The only way to lose weight and keep it off in a healthy way is to reduce your calories and to exercise more. An important tip to remember is to ask yourself as you start to eat something, "Am I eating this because I need it or because it's there?" Another important factor is that you don't base your self-worth on your physical appearance but on your personhood.

- *Did you get eight hours of sleep per night most nights this week?*

Many people boast that they can get by on little sleep, yet studies show that most adults need about eight hours of sleep per night to function at their best and to stay healthy. Children need even more. For example, an elementary school child may need ten or eleven hours, a junior high school student nine or ten, and a high school student eight to nine. Some elderly people, however, can get by on less than eight hours.

When we don't have enough sleep, we tend to be irritable, more critical, more depressed, have a harder time concentrating, work less efficiently, and enjoy life less. Sleep is essential to sound mental, emotional, and spiritual health.

- *How much of a "Type A" personality are you?*

As noted before, a "Type A" individual is one who is time oriented, yet never seems to have enough time. He tends to be competitive and success-oriented, a workaholic, often doing two or more things at once. This type of personality may experience a great deal of underlying anger behind the success orientation and have a strong need to produce in order to feel successful. Such individuals are prone to heart disease and, statistically, are more likely to die young.

It is important for the Type A personality to slow down, relax, and put his priorities in proper order. Type A personalities tend to move, walk, and eat rapidly. They also tend to hurry those with whom they are talking. Type A's get upset when waiting and when they must perform repetitive tasks. They try to schedule things tighter and tighter in order to get more things done. Even taking a short break from work or taking time to relax and do nothing can produce guilt in a Type A.

Since Type A persons usually live life on a schedule—a tight schedule—they must rearrange that schedule to include time to relax, time for meditation, time with children and mate, time just to goof off, and *after* all that, their scheduled time for work. For most people, of course, that will involve the normal forty-hour work week, and when absolutely necessary up to fifty hours—but no more. Then, after rearranging their schedule according to priorities, they must determine to follow it.

If you are a Type A, you need to develop an ability to slow down. To do that, become aware of your need to take life slower. Take deep, slow breaths to aid in the slowing down process. Review your priorities and be determined to be content with completing or accomplishing perhaps half as many tasks a day as you have been accustomed to trying to do, remembering that taking care of yourself and the physical and emotional needs of your loved ones is your first priority. For some, that means getting away for a while; for others, it means saying no to heading up that committee yet another year. Each of us is responsible for finding ways to be responsible toward himself.

LEARN TIME MANAGEMENT SKILLS

To spend less pressured time with work, time management skills may need to be sharpened. Will Rogers once said, "It's not so much what you do each day, it's what gets done that counts." Although this is not a book on time management, some practical suggestions are in order.

- *Take inventory of your usage of time.*

Invest time in scheduling, making lists of things to be accomplished, and prioritizing that list. Plan ahead, allowing sufficient time for interruptions. Beware of "time bandits," those things that intrude into your schedule and rob you of precious minutes and hours that could be used to accomplish the task at hand.

- *Learn to concentrate on the task at hand.*

Work at screening out distractions. Learn to distinguish between essential details and nonessentials.

- *Learn to grasp the big picture.*

Work at "majoring on the majors." Be sure to relate your daily tasks to overall life goals and even to one-year and five-year goals.

- *Work at being decisive.*

Get all the information available, and then make a decision. Don't put off deciding. Avoid procrastination.

- *Learn to delegate, particularly those things that can be done effectively by other people.*

Don't spread yourself too thin. Concentrate your time and energies on doing those few things you are best at doing.

Making changes in all these physical areas of your life will take time. However, as you start them, you will begin to find the physical strength to start making other changes as well.

NOTE

1. Dr. Howard Hendricks, unpublished class notes.

14
STARTING THE UPWARD SPIRAL EMOTIONALLY

Before addressing those things you can do to take care of yourself emotionally, we must address an emotional problem of the most severe burnout victim, that of suicidal thinking.

REVERSING SUICIDAL THINKING

Some time ago a woman phoned in to our radio talk show to tell us about her daughter who had been feeling burned out and depressed. The depression had become a major one. She had voiced suicidal thoughts to her family on several occasions, but they had not taken her seriously. Eventually, the daughter killed herself. The woman who phoned in did so to warn listeners to take seriously the suicidal thoughts of loved ones.

Anyone who is talking about suicide or who admits to having suicidal thoughts should be under professional care, preferably by a psychiatrist or psychologist. To the severely depressed who have lost hope, suicide may seem the only way out of their situation. Anyone who has a "suicide plan" should be hospitalized immediately.

One common misconception involves the fear that to mention suicide to a depressed person will bring about thoughts that have not occurred previously or will increase the likelihood of a suicide attempt. Actually, to lovingly confront a person with a question about suicidal thoughts can be the first step toward reversing suicidal thinking. This was the case with the depressed salesman, Mr. I, whose pastor raised the question with him. Mr. I then spent four weeks in the hospital under our care. He was able to reverse his burnout and depression and to put his marriage and life back together.

In our clinic we have developed ten warning signs of individuals who are most likely to attempt suicide. Several of these, as you will notice, have a close relationship with burnout.

Warning signs of suicide:

1. Intense emotional pain, as seen in severe depression
2. Intense feelings of hopelessness
3. A prior history of a suicide attempt or voiced warnings of suicidal intentions
4. Severe health problems
5. A significant loss—death of a spouse, loss of a job, and so on
6. Forming a suicide plan
7. Chronic self-destructive behavior—alcoholism, an eating disorder, and so on
8. An intense need to achieve
9. An excess of disturbing life events within the previous six months
10. Someone who is single, male, white, and more than forty-five years of age, who has experienced some of the above signs

TAKING CARE OF SELF—EMOTIONALLY

If your burnout has not reached the severe stage of suicidal thinking, our "Taking Care of Yourself" test includes a number of steps you can take personally to help reverse the emotional part of your burnout.

- *Have you laughed several times today?*

Laughter is a sign of good mental health. Medical studies indicate that laughter releases chemicals called endorphins in the brain, promoting feelings of well-being. Author Norman Cousins helped himself recover from a debilitating disease by watching old film comedies and cartoons, allowing himself to laugh every day as part of his healing process. The absence of frequent laughter may be an external symptom indicating the presence of deeper emotional conflicts.

- *What percentage of your self-talk was positive today?*

Each of us talks to himself. The way in which we talk to ourselves has a great deal to do with how we feel. Self-talk that is negative, derogatory, or critical fosters depression. Make an effort to be more positive, kind, and forgiving in the things you say to yourself. Why not set aside a time to consider how you talk to yourself? Look for specific changes. Forgive yourself when necessary and move on from personal failures.

- *What amount of time this past week did you spend living in the present?*

Many people focus on past failures or past accomplishments. Either extreme can be damaging to good mental health. Often when we are depressed, we focus on the past. It is important that we live in the here and now.

Another misplaced focus involves dwelling only on what may happen in the future. Anxiety causes a misplaced focus on the possible problems of tomorrow. Tomorrow will take care of itself.

Learn to deal with your past, look forward to your future, and live properly one day at a time in the here and now.

- *Did you do something three times this week for relaxation and recreation?*

Maintaining good mental health often involves learning to relax. We have found it worthwhile to plan at least three times a week activities specifically dedicated to enjoyable recreation, something not connected with your usual line of work. If you are experiencing burnout or near burnout, try some new recreational and relaxing activities, other than your usual, since they obviously are not helping your situation.

That is particularly true of the one who views a lot of television, trying to forget the worries of the day through watching the traumas of make-believe characters. Watching make-believe, or even someone else's real life, is never a substitute for experiencing life yourself. Instead, shoot some baskets with your kids or play some table games with the whole family. Try those activities for fun, without a highly competitive attitude. Occasionally, you might even play less than your best in order to let the other person win. It will be good for his or her self-esteem and sense of pleasure, and for your sense of values.

If a job or vocation is exceedingly stressful, tiring, frustrating, or boring over a long period of time, perhaps a change in responsibilities, activities, job, or career needs to be considered. If possible, a sabbatical may be in order. But make sure the change is to positive types of activities as well as less demanding ones. Don't act on a burnout impulse to become a full-time hermit, beach bum, or occasional tinkerer.

For two of our case examples, considering a job change brought different decisions.

Dan, the eighteen-year-old factory worker, Dan, did go back to his old job temporarily. Meanwhile, he received vocational testing at our clinic and found that he had abilities in other areas. Also he discovered that his type of personality would not tolerate a monotonous job. (Some people can do monotonous work and even seem to thrive on it. They block out the monotony and seem to enjoy themselves. Other people need new and different challenges.)

Eventually, Dan quit his job and began work as a carpenter, where he could do different things each day and see the work of his hands begin to make a house take shape. Only when he changed jobs to one more compatible with his personality did Dan recover completely from his burnout.

Jeanne, the mental health worker who counseled depressed people, was encouraged to take a different tack. To continue working in such a specific and difficult area, she found that thirty hours of cases a week, instead of her former fifty to sixty hours, was all she could handle effectively. She was then able to spend more time in relaxation and volunteer work. A change of pace and rearranging her schedule, rather than a change of job, was the key to reversing her burnout.

Although a certain amount of stress is necessary and even good in life, our response to stress can make us capable of handling the necessary stresses of life more successfully. And although removing as much stress as possible may be necessary to recover from current burnout, stress management needs to be learned to avoid future burnout. That involves:

- learning when it is appropriate to say no, both to yourself and to others who may place demands on you
- learning when it is appropriate to settle for limited objectives
- being able to distinguish between situations in which you should respond with your "flight or fight" defense mechanism and those in which you should take a less concerned approach

We must learn to recognize our human limitations, and when we sense that we are close to our limit, take a deep breath, relax, and seek—at least temporarily—a change of pace, a change of place, a change of perspective. If you think you can't afford a vacation, then make it a financial priority and plan and budget for it.

- *How often were you stuck on "Plan A" this month?*

"Plan A" is your routine schedule. It includes all the things you normally do each day from the time you get up until the time you go to bed. Plan A includes the events of your day, your activities, your habits, and your appearance. People often become depressed because they are following Plan A.

If your Plan A is leading to frequent bouts with burnout and depression, it may be time to form a Plan B. That may involve coming up with five to ten specific things you can do in a given period of time, say a week, to change how you feel.

The recreational activities mentioned above could be a part of that. Other changes to your plan may include rearranging your before-work activities. If you feel sluggish until you eat breakfast, eat breakfast when you first get up. If you have trouble keeping your eyes open first thing in the morning, take a shower first. If finding something to wear each morning is a great frustration, start laying out clothes the night before. Plan B should also include refreshing Sundays or whatever day you have off.

When developing Plan B, include one meaningful social contact each day, by phone if necessary. Develop a daily routine that includes some variety and is personally satisfying, if only in the little things. People who are emotionally oriented tend to become bored quickly. Variety in daily life helps that.

- *How much change have you experienced during the past year?*

Because of the mobile society in which we live, change is a major factor in life. Changes in residence, employment, or schools all produce stress points. Medical studies show that if too many stress points accumulate during any one year, there is a great likelihood of developing significant physical or emotional problems. The Holmes-Rahe Stress Test was designed to identify the number and severity of stress factors experienced by an individual during the preceding year. A total of 200 or more stress points can indicate the presence or likelihood of burnout.

THE STRESS OF ADJUSTING TO CHANGES*

Events	Scale of Impact
Death of a spouse	100
Divorce	73
Marital separation	65
Jail term	63
Death of close family member	63
Personal injury or illness	53
Marriage	50
Fired at work	47
Marital reconciliation	45
Retirement	45
Change in health of family member	44
Pregnancy	40
Sex difficulties	39
Gain of new family member	39
Business readjustment	39
Change in financial state	38
Death of close friend	37
Change to different line of work	36
Change in number of arguments with spouse	35
Mortgage over $10,000	31

* Reprinted with permission from T. H. Holmes and R. H. Rahe, "The Social Adjustment Rating Scale," *Journal of Psychosomatic Research* 2:213. Copyright 1967, Pergamon Press.

THE STRESS OF ADJUSTING TO CHANGES (cont.)

Events	Scale of Impact
Foreclosure of mortgage or loan	30
Change in responsibilities at work	29
Son or daughter leaving home	29
Trouble with in-laws	29
Outstanding personal achievement	28
Wife begins or stops work	26
Begin or end school	26
Change in living conditions	25
Revision of personal habits	24
Trouble with boss	23
Change in work hours or conditions	20
Change in residence	20
Change in schools	19
Change in recreation	19
Change in church activities	19
Change in social activities	18
Mortgage or loan less than $10,000	17
Change in sleeping habits	16
Change in number of family get-togethers	15
Change in eating habits	15
Vacation	13
Christmas	12
Minor violations of the law	11

• *Is the sexual part of your life healthy?*

Proper sexual function plays a role in preventing burnout.

There are two important principles to remember.

Since we are male and female, it is both normal and desirable for husbands and wives to enjoy the romance and excitement of marital love.

Sexual misconduct will produce serious consequences.

For the married person that means remaining true to one's mate not only physically but in thought, word, and deed.

For the single person, that involves a discipline and commitment to purity. Public opinion seems to indicate that a majority of adults—61 percent, including 78 percent of young adults, according to a recent Roper Organization survey—now believe that premarital sex is not morally wrong. That, however, does not change the negative feelings premarital sex produces. Those include feelings of unease, frustration, and guilt—real guilt—which involves holding back, a less than complete and unending commitment to the present and future well-being of the other person. As Dick Purnell says in *Becoming a Friend and Lover*, in the marriage relationship

> there is safety and security . . . without fear of abandonment. There is also total freedom from guilt in sex . . . Outside of marriage, guilt eats away at the individuals until the relationship is either destroyed or crippled. . . . Stimulated by lifetime commitment and the absence of guilt . . . we are able to be ourselves totally and to be emotionally "naked" without fear. . . . When we have sex outside the boundaries that God has set up for our protection and provision, we end up cheating ourselves.[1]

Feelings of unease, frustration, and guilt, plus fears related to AIDS and other sexually transmitted diseases, produce added stress in a single person's life instead of relieving it. We have observed similar feelings in married individuals who engage in extramarital sex. The added stress of a sexual relationship without a lifetime commitment adds to those factors that can create burnout and make it harder to recover from burnout. Moral principles to govern sex are meant as a protection (physically, emotionally, and spiritually), not as a limitation to our pleasure and fulfillment.

For singles, maintaining sexual purity and learning how to relate to others in close friendships before marriage alleviates stress and burnout, as Purnell's statement so aptly shows. For married couples, maintaining marital romance and cultivating the sparkle of an intimate relationship can add zest to life and help prevent burnout.

- *Have you done something good—physically, psychologically, or spiritually—for one person this week?*

We are living in a self-involved generation. The selfish spirit of this age can be mentally unhealthy. Physically, you could help someone with chores or errands. Psychologically, you might provide someone with counsel or just a listening ear. Spiritually, you might tell a friend what lessons you have learned recently. We are emotionally enriched when we invest ourselves in others.

- *Have you forgiven the last three people who offended you?*

Forgiveness is important because, if we don't forgive others, we tend to turn our anger inward, which leads to bitterness,then depression. Forgiveness involves, by an act of the will, choosing to no longer hold a grudge against an offending party. It is inaccurate to say, "I cannot forgive." Since forgiveness is a matter of the will, we can say, "I will forgive." It is important when we are offended to quickly choose to forgive, rather than to harbor grudges.

- *How many times has envy affected you this year?*

Harboring envy toward others leads to depression. A proper response to the success of others is to be happy for them. When we strive to prove that we are more important than others, which is the basis for envy, we are like a person chasing the wind, which is futile. It is important to be grateful for whatever we have received. When envy surfaces, remember that in one sense none of us deserves anything. Whatever we get from life is a gift.

- *Did you talk with your spouse (or, if single, a close friend or relative) three times this week about your feelings?*

Emotional problems often result when we repress our feelings instead of dealing with them. It is important to sit down with our spouse (or roommate or close friend) and share both the good and bad events of the day. Shared feelings also is important for resolving areas of marital conflict. Men generally tend to hide their feelings more than women and may need to work specifically on this area.

Tips for conflict resolution include:

- Use "I" messages—"I feel," "I need," "I want"—instead of "you" statements—"you should," "you shouldn't."
- Avoid attacking each other's character; explain only the specific behavior that offends.
- Ask for some kind of specific change, keep the issues to the present, and avoid bringing up the past.

- Listen to your spouse.
- Don't let your emotions get out of hand.
- Resist the temptation to keep track of who won past conflicts. Recognize that when someone "wins" a marital conflict, everyone loses.
- Ask for and give feedback to each other.
- Schedule time to discuss feelings with your mate.

- *Did you share your burdens with a friend this week?*

A successful, intelligent, hard-working businessman suffered a major heart attack. During his recovery he become close friends with one of us. During a telephone conversation, he remarked, "You are about the only person I feel I can really call a close friend." What is remarkable about his statement is that his experience typifies that of many candidates for burnout.

Many people who experience depression or burnout do not have even one friend to whom they are close enough to share their personal feelings and still feel loved and accepted. An important step in maintaining an emotional balance is to develop close friendships. Each of us needs about six people with whom we can share our true feelings and still feel loved. It is hard for any person, even a mate, to carry the full burden of all our feelings, particularly if he or she is going through an emotionally heavy period, too.

Of course, if you are already in burnout, building a friendship may be hard to do. If someone offers friendship and unconditional understanding at this time, don't rebuff it. It's what you need, even if you have little emotional energy to offer in return. Allow others to give friendship to you. After you recover from burnout, the give and take of friendships will be important to keeping your life balanced.

If you still have the emotional energy, start looking for friends who will be good listeners, who will be loyal, and who will care, but also who will be willing to give a viewpoint different from yours if they think it is needed. Find someone with whom you can relate, then spend time with that person developing a growing friendship and building mutual trust.

Beginning a relationship may involve challenging another person to become involved with you in helping balance each other's lives. If you both need to reduce your weight, you might agree to call each other every evening to list what you have eaten that day. If you need to spend more quality time with family members, work out a similar reporting arrangement with someone from your workplace, church, or neighborhood. Such a reporting system, often called accountability, may help you achieve personal change, provide a helping hand to someone else, and develop a casual relationship into a closer friendship, all at the same time.

- *Did you do at least one specific thing this week to become closer to a relative—a parent, brother, sister, or other near kin?*

Each of us has a family heritage, one that has tremendous bearing on our mental health. Often there is a need to go back and mend or repair relationships, building a new way of relating that can lead to mental and emotional stability. It is important to take the initiative to build a closer relationship with your family, rather than waiting on others in the family to take the lead. Doing at least one thing per week—perhaps a phone call, a letter, a visit, or an outing—with extended family members can build closer relationships and foster emotional health.

ACTIONS LEAD TO EMOTIONS

If you see a number of areas above that need changing in your life, you may think, *But I don't feel like doing all that!* particularly if you are already feeling the effects of burnout. However, an important principle of improving our life is that proper actions lead to proper emotions. We frequently find that true in our counseling. The most dramatic illustration is, perhaps, in marital counseling. Often a husband or wife will say, "I don't feel like trying any more. I've lost that feeling of love for my mate." In such cases, our counsel is to *act* as if you love your spouse, and soon you will begin to *feel* as if you love your mate. Many initially respond with unbelief but later return to acknowledge that the approach works.

The same approach can work in your relationship with others and even with yourself. Begin taking some of those needed steps to revitalize your life, to begin to reverse that burnout spiral, whether you feel like doing them or not. The actions of doing the right thing will soon be followed by the desire to do them, and you'll be on the upward spiral, moving away from the depths of burnout.

NOTE

1. Dick Purnell, *Becoming a Friend and Lover* (San Bernardino, Calif.: Here's Life, 1986), pp. 58-59.

15
REACHING BALANCE
OR BURNOUT?

A counselor was invited to address the annual meeting of a large mental health facility in northern Illinois. The subject was the relationship between stress and obsessive behavior. As the speaker walked into the facility where the meeting was being held, he was met by the mental health administrator who said, "Do I need to hear what you have to say! I hope you have some practical suggestions for getting a handle on my own stress and obsessiveness."

That desire has been voiced to us by individuals from all walks of life. Many obsessives suffer periodic obsessive-compulsive disorders, receive counseling, and are aware of their unbalanced obsessive behavior. But they realize that simply understanding the problem, or even tracing it to its early childhood origin, doesn't do anything to reverse it.

Put another way, most perfectionists find that insight into the nature of their difficulties is not sufficient to effect change. We have found a total revamping of *attitudes* to be necessary, including gaining insight into thought processes, developing interpersonal relational skills, and acquiring the motivation to change.

Some counselors say the way to overcome extreme obsessive-compulsive behavior is to remove all structure from counseling. Instead of giving specific direction, the counselor should simply provide support and encouragement. But the problem with that approach is that O-Cs have difficulty expressing their feelings, so they tend to be more comfortable with a high degree of structure. Often a counselor will simply try to get an obsessive-compulsive to remove all structure and organization from his or her life; however, the real issue is not structure or lack of it but an inability to get in touch with personal feelings. Removing all structure from the obsessive's life can actually hinder the process of balancing obsessive behavior.

STEPS TO OVERCOMING O-C BEHAVIOR

Driven by his perfectionism and a penchant for control, a perfectionist is at high risk of burnout. Frequently unhappy with himself, those around him, and with circumstances, his expectations can set him up for increased risk.

The most important thing a perfectionist can do is gain insight into his hidden emotions. That will involve breaking through the denial that creates the climate in which perfectionism and workaholism grow. As Peters and Waterman point out in *In Search of Excellence,* we all struggle with self-deception. "In a recent psychological study, when a random study of male adults were asked to rate themselves on 'the ability to get along with others,' ALL subjects, 100%, put themselves in the top half of the population, 60% rated themselves in the top 10% of the population, and a full 25% ever so humbly thought they were in the top 1% of the population."[1]

We all like to think we're tops, that we're in control, that we have no problems—and although we certainly need to be encouraged and to take a positive view of ourselves, it's also important that we realistically avoid the denial that covers up the underlying causes of our perfectionism and workaholism. We need to pay attention to the effects of our personality type and deal with early environment factors (those unmet, idealistic expectations left over from childhood). As Mark Twain once pointed out, "It's not what you eat that destroys you; it's what eats you." Once we gain insight into our denial and the related perfectionism and control issues, there are practical steps we can take to balance our perfectionism.

• *Learn to give and receive unconditional love.*

Some time ago the following slogan was printed in *The Ladies Home Journal:* "Those who love deeply never grow old. They may die of old age, but they die young."

It's important to recognize what this kind of love involves. It's not simply a feeling or an emotion. It's a choice, a decision, an act of the will. It doesn't simply desire to be close to another; it desires what is best for another. It has another's interest at heart. It doesn't simply prefer what's good for another. It's literally willing to go to the point of sacrifice. That's the kind of love we need to learn to give and receive.

The atom is the fundamental building block of our physical universe. Love is the fundamental building block of relationships. Two hundred years ago a well-known encyclopedia used only four lines to discuss the word *atom,* whereas it devoted five pages to a discussion of *love.* However, a recent edition of the same encyclopedia devoted five pages to discussing the word *atom. Love* was omitted. No wonder our universe is so populated with perfectionists.[2]

- *Develop accountability in a relationship based on love and mutual respect.*

The perfectionist is by nature a loner who has difficulty with accountability. He holds himself and others to an exacting standard. He needs healthy, balanced individuals—a spouse, a few close friends of the same sex—with whom he can be incredibly honest, particularly in the area of perfectionism and workaholism.

- *Improve your ability to relate to others.*

Although unbalanced obsessives tend to take a "lone ranger" approach to life, even the Lone Ranger found it important to depend upon his faithful sidekick, Tonto, when facing adversity.

We see two aspects of this "people factor."

Develop a network of significant people for support. Developing friendships is an active, not a passive, matter. Because imbalanced obsessives tend to be more task-oriented than people-oriented, this is an area to which they need to devote themselves. Look for people with whom you are like-minded, people with whom you share values, interests, and goals. Work at accepting them unconditionally, that is, "giving them some slack," when they don't live up to your expectations. Treat them with the time-tested Golden Rule, as you would like them to treat you—*not* in the way you feel they have actually treated you. Loyalty and love, extended even in times of adversity, are the soil in which friendships grow.

Several of us have adopted a personal goal of developing one good friendship every two to three years. Frank Minirth says, "I find that I cannot develop really close friendships any more quickly than this. Developing good friends is hard work. But I've also discovered that having good friends with whom I can share my feelings is essential to my own mental and spiritual well-being."

Sometimes it can be helpful for O-Cs to develop or become part of support groups designed for the purpose of sharing friendships. One of us has been involved for some years with a group of obsessive-compulsives known as OCWA—the "Obsessive-Compulsive Workaholics Anonymous." Started informally, it has provided both mutual support and a number of mental health-producing laughs as well. Perhaps OCWA chapters will spring up in other places around the country.

Learn to communicate feelings. For the obsessive, communicating facts is easier than expressing emotions. "I feel" messages are almost like a foreign language to many O-Cs. We suggest that obsessives establish a specific time to share feelings with their spouse and have an agreement with a few good friends, in the context of unconditional love, to feel free to express feelings whenever they need to do so.

- *Get to know and accept yourself.*

Get to know yourself, accept yourself, and become all that you can be.

We need to come to a realistic appraisal of our personality, abilities, and unique design. The clearest and most obvious danger is to think of ourselves more highly than we should. But many of us react to the other extreme and spend a lot of time putting ourselves down.

Here is a practical suggestion: take a sizable chunk of time, sit down, reflect on yourself, and make a list of your strengths and abilities. Perhaps you are highly organized. Maybe you are a self-starter. Perhaps you have an ability to grasp intellectual material. You may be an excellent communicator. Write down those strengths. Then begin listing ways you can improve them.

When U.S. Senator Bill Bradley was in high school, he worked one summer on Capitol Hill. Each evening he stopped by a high school gym. He picked out six or eight spots on the court from which to shoot baskets, and he wouldn't leave until he had made fifty shots from each. Bradley became an excellent shot, and his hard work and patience paid off. He ultimately became an All-American at Princeton University and a highly successful professional basketball player for the New York Knicks before he ran for Congress.

One of the obsessive-compulsive's greatest strengths is a willingness to work. We suggest that obsessives pay attention not only to strengthening strengths but also to working hard on their weaknesses —even harder than they do on their strengths. These may include handling emotions, accepting and loving people unconditionally, or organizing areas of their lives that tend to escape order altogether. Whatever the weakness, the obsessive must work on it diligently.

- *Surrender your life to God's control.*

If you have not trusted Jesus Christ as your personal Savior and Lord, acknowledge that to do so is not only the key to overcoming burnout but also the ultimate answer to meaning and purpose in life.

Acknowledge to God that you are a sinner (that you have not and cannot, on your own, live up to His desires for your life) and that you yourself cannot bridge the gap that your sins have caused between you and God. Realize that Christ's death was the punishment you deserve for your sins. Because He took your punishment upon Himself, His death and resurrection became the basis for the forgiveness of your sins and for your coming into a close and completed relationship with God. Depend on His death and resurrection to cancel your debt to God.

Trust Him as your personal Savior from a life, here and eternally, without God. Realize that His Holy Spirit then resides in your life to lead you, comfort you, empower you, and allow you to feel God's love for you.

It is worth the effort to work to recapture joy in personally communicating with God through Bible reading and study.

- *Forgive yourself for not being perfect.*

After all, none of us is. It's difficult to learn that perhaps less than perfect may be just as right as "perfect." Exercise the virtues of tolerance and forbearance toward yourself and others. Learn to live one day at a time, not dwelling on your past mistakes or on harmful actions that were initiated against you, or focusing on the future, wondering what is going to happen next.

- *Learn to give up grudges and bitterness, choosing to forgive those toward whom you are bitter, even if they don't deserve forgiveness.*

The emotional energy used to harbor unresolved grudges and feelings of anger can often be redirected to useful pursuits surprisingly quickly when burnout victims *choose* to make peace with their emotions by forgiving those people who have let them down.

- *Learn to discover your personal significance not in your performance but in your relationships.*

A sign in the office of a successful business executive reads "Who I am is far more important than what I do." One day a new manager hired by that executive—the chief operating officer of a nationally recognized corporation—took exception to the motto on the manager's wall. His argument, "It's far more important that we all perform. That's what we're here for."

After several years, through good times and adversities, the manager one day walked into the office of the man who had hired him. Pointing to the motto on the wall, he said, "About that motto —I'm finally coming to see things the way you do. Working with you has been a good experience for me. I've been challenged to excellence, and I've been acknowledged when I did well. More important, I've been accepted for who I am, respected as a person apart from my performance. That's made it a lot easier to handle the difficult things. I felt accepted, respected as a person." It is important that we find our significance in our person, not in our performance.

When we realize where our true significance lies we will be free to deal with current causes of stress, including a frantic schedule of "burning the candle at both ends and in the middle." Many people have found it necessary to quit one of the two full-time jobs they were trying to sustain, or to take a less demanding position, even at lower pay, and found their personal worth didn't suffer at all.

- *Learn to recognize distorted thinking and change it.*

Balancing obsessive behavior also involves correcting the flaws in our thinking. According to Chris Thurman in *The Lies We Believe,* a good place to start is to notice carefully our "self-talk," comparing it with inaccurate things or lies we tell ourselves.[3]

We sometimes suggest that obsessives keep a daily written record of self-critical thoughts and statements, or that they ask a spouse or close friend to hold them accountable for their self-talk. Sometimes self-talk habits become automatic thoughts. When obsessives write them down, they are able to pinpoint inaccuracies and develop more objective and appropriate ways to talk to themselves.

Four of the more common unhealthy messages we give ourselves are:

"I must be perfect."
"I should please others."
"I must try harder."
"Life must be fair."

For example, Jeanne, a graduate student, faced a Monday deadline on a paper, and she had a major exam. However, family and work responsibilities caused her to have an extremely busy weekend with very little time for preparation. On Monday Jeanne hit the panic button.

Under those circumstances, hitting the panic button was not necessarily a bad thing to do. However, undergirding Jeanne's thinking was the feeling, *I've failed miserably. I didn't get my studying done this weekend. I allowed my schedule to get out of control. I'm a failure as a person. I'm a failure as a student. I will fail in the future.*

Furthermore, as she typed her paper Jeanne made several mistakes. Again, in her personal self-assessment, this was an unpardonable sin. Her thoughts: *The professor will certainly notice all these errors. He will think the paper is poorly thought out. He'll consider me an irresponsible student. He'll be sure I don't really care about doing well. I'll probably wind up with an F, or a D at best.*

Although we might be quick to recognize the "all or nothing" inaccuracy in Jeanne's thinking (she had some of the highest marks in the class), we may have a tendency to fall into the same trap of irrational thinking ourselves.

Correcting the flaws in our thinking involves an awareness, even though it may be painful, of the defense mechanisms we use to deceive ourselves. As we discussed earlier, some common defense mechanisms are: *intellectualization* to avoid facing our emotions; *magical thinking* to fool ourselves into trying to do more than we can accomplish; *reaction formation* to develop acceptable attitudes and behavior to hide our lustful, greedy, or power-hungry thoughts from ourselves and from others; *undoing* to compensate for the unacknowledged anger we feel toward others; *isolation* to separate flawed areas of our lives from the reality we perceive about ourselves. It is imperative that we come to grips with these flaws in our thinking.

Facing distorted thinking is difficult for practicing obsessives. The following checklist by Aaron Beck can help an obsessive recognize the distorted way he looks at reality:

> Magnification—making a mountain out of a molehill
> Personalization—relating everything that happens to yourself
> Polarization—seeing everything in black and white, including nonabsolutes
> Overgeneralization—making blanket judgments or predictions on the basis of a single incident
> Selective abstraction—focusing on a single detail out of context
> Emotional reasoning—treating facts as feelings[4]

One of the most important keys to overcoming imbalanced obsessive *behavior* is to correct imbalanced obsessive *thinking*. Balanced thinking will lead to balanced living.

● *Learn to be assertive.*

Frequently, an O-C's problem is either an inability to say no or the inability to say no graciously. Obsessives tend to adopt extreme "either/or" thinking; therefore, they are either passive, allowing others to run them over, or they become aggressive after "taking it" for a long time, lashing out at the people and circumstances producing the stress. A balanced approach to handling stress involves the right degree of assertiveness.

Assertiveness is the ability to stand up for one's rights, to express one's true feelings when appropriate—without fear of reprisal, to be able to say no to unreasonable demands, and to request the things one needs and deserves.

Foundational to appropriate assertiveness is the basic underlying message "I count, and you count." If we refuse to be assertive, we are either saying, "I count, and you don't count" (which is aggressiveness), or, "You count, but I don't count" (which is nonassertiveness or passivity). The following list of assertive statements can help obsessive-compulsives and others who need to become more balanced in this area.

"No, I won't do that."   "I think you're not being fair."
"That makes me angry."   "I need something from you."
"I disagree with you."   "Thank you, but I don't care to."
"This really bothers me."   "It hurts my feelings when you
"Please stop doing that."   say things like that."
"Will you help me?"   "There are some things I think
"I really like that   we need to get straightened
  about you."   out."

- *Conduct a time inventory with a view toward establishing a balanced schedule that allows time not only for work but for relationships, relaxation, and fun. See that you get proper exercise, rest, and diet.*

Realistically assess your goals and schedules. Learn to set strict time limits for work projects. Develop the technique of keeping a desk drawer into which current work can be placed. Walk away when it's time to walk away from the work. For the perfectionist, it will be be difficult to leave work to be completed another time. For some individuals, for example, the procrastinator, incomplete work is a pattern of life. In fact, for some perfectionists, this is a perpetual problem.

An obsessive can become a truly balanced, highly productive individual—one who relates effectively to other people. He can do so by establishing daily priorities consistent with his life goals, by learning to distinguish the important from the urgent.

Although many obsessives tend to overdo time management, they sometimes ignore good time management principles, including preparing for future events. Because they are so successful at being achievement-oriented, they leave unfinished tasks for the last minute, assuming they have the ability to accomplish in minutes what takes other people hours and days. Type A O-Cs often see themselves as almost superhuman. Unfortunately, unforeseen snags are likely to trip them up. We have discovered through personal experience the wisdom of the old proverb "An ounce of prevention is worth a pound of cure."

Delegate to others when possible. One of the obsessive's favorite sayings is "Thanks, but I'd rather do it myself." That's not usually an appropriately assertive response (although it can be under certain circumstances). Usually it indicates an unwillingness to relinquish control.

- *Learn to live in the present*

Learn to live life one day at a time. Because obsessives tend to be people of extremes, they frequently find themselves living in the past, plagued with guilt, or they find themselves living in the future. They are anxious about what tomorrow may bring, and that intense anxiety distracts them.

The realistic obsessive-compulsive learns to live without being haunted by the past or overly concerned about the future. In other words, if life gives you a hot fudge sundae, eat it without feeling guilty, but avoid gluttony.

- *Make an advantage/disadvantage list.*

Make a list of the advantages and disadvantages of perfectionism. Then weigh the benefits against the costs. In this way you can call into play familiar and often-used skills to help assess their perfectionism.

The process will hopefully bring about an awareness, perhaps for the first time, that perfectionism or obsessive-compulsive behaviors do not always produce positive results. That awareness, in turn, can give you the motivation to give up the imbalances in obsessiveness.

One obsessive came up with the following interesting lists.

Advantages:
Obsessive behavior helps me produce quality work.
It also helps me produce a greater quantity of work.

Disadvantages:
I'm often so uptight I have trouble producing quality work.
My rigidity and perfectionism tend to stifle my creativity and my willingness to try novel approaches.
I constantly find myself criticizing myself and others. That takes all the fun out of relationships and the rest of my life.
I have trouble walking away from my responsibility. In fact, I sometimes have trouble relaxing.

Conclusion: To be an imbalanced perfectionist is counterproductive.

- *Discover less obsessive ways to handle the stress factors in your life.*

Again, a list or other form of written evaluation can be helpful. Write down various stress factors, both major and minor, and then decide which ones you can influence and which you have no control over.

- *One final step: Learn to moderate control, even give up control.*

Perfectionists attempt to "play God," often trying to change circumstances that are far beyond their ability to affect, much less change. Remember the famous serenity prayer: "God grant me the serenity to accept the things I cannot change, the courage to change the things I can, and the wisdom to know the difference." When this prayer becomes a vital part of the life of a perfectionist, balance is within sight.

NOTES

1. Thomas Peters and Robert Waterman, *In Search of Excellence* (New York: Harper & Row, 1982), p. 56.
2. Paul Lee Tan, ed., *Encyclopedia of 7700 Illustrations* (Rockville, Md.: Assurance, 1979). p. 759.
3. Chris Thurman, *The Lies We Believe* (Nashville: Thomas Nelson, 1989), pp. 35-57.
4. David Burns, *Feeling Good: The New Need Therapy* (New York: Signet, 1980). Cited in *The Lies We Believe,* pp. 109-19.

16

RELATING POSITIVELY TO OTHERS

Recently a young man appeared in our office to interview for a job opening in a new clinic that was being established in a nearby city. During the course of the interview, he asserted, "Here's how I operate. Give me a job to do, and I'll do it. I'm the kind of person who likes to know what's expected of me, to whom I'm responsible, and how soon I need to get a job done. If there's one phrase that characterizes me it's 'I am responsible.'"

The two of us present with the young man looked at each other and smiled as we thought the same thing, *Ah ha! Another obsessive-compulsive personality!*

Since this book is written about balancing obsessive-compulsive traits (which are not bad in themselves), it is important to recognize that one of the major strengths of the obsessive-compulsive is his conscientiousness about duty. Yet our main duty generally involves relating to others.

In this chapter, we shall seek to move beyond correcting the problems we have in relating to people and address the positive. In addition, we will seek to present workable principles for building and maintaining positive relationships.

Living a balanced, healthy life is not something that can be achieved in isolation. No less an authority than Dr. Karl Menninger, who has been described as knowing more about the subject of mental health than any other living person, offers the following perspective on a mentally healthy individual:

Indeed, when we wish to find out how well Mr. X is integrated, we do not check his performance randomly at any odd level and leave it at that, but we try to formulate an organized statement about his over-all functioning with an ultimate emphasis on his topmost performances: how he gets along with other people, how "whole" he is, how well he can adapt himself to the demands of the day, how well he can master his inner and outer environment to the benefit of himself and society.[1]

Relating to others is often a difficult area for the burnout-prone obsessive-compulsive. However, before focusing on human relationships, it is necessary to be able to relate appropriately to God. Many centuries ago Jesus Christ offered a perspective that provided His hearers with a way to evaluate overall human functioning but that, significantly, included another element—the vertical relationship with man's Creator.

In essence, Jesus was saying that our ultimate responsibility is to love—to wholeheartedly love God and unconditionally love people. And He classified this responsibility as of overwhelming importance: "There is no commandment greater than these."

FORGIVENESS

Having a forgiving attitude is also crucial for building close relationships. The individual who is forgiving will maintain emotional and spiritual tenderness, instead of developing a hard edge. Individuals who refuse to forgive, and harbor feelings of ill will, resentment, and bitterness, can become "hard-hearted." Obsessive-compulsive individuals, who by nature tend to avoid relating on an emotional level, often struggle in this area. Yet the consequences of refusing to forgive are far too grave to neglect.

Forgiveness is neither cheap nor easy. Yet we try to avoid that reality, falling at times into certain traps. One of those traps is to forgive without dealing with the issue. We counseled a man whose son had become involved in all kinds of problems, including drugs and stealing. The father was always willing to forgive, but he never faced head-on the reality of his son's destructive behavior.

Similarly, a wife who sought our counsel claimed to have forgiven her husband for being unfaithful. But she forgave him conditionally. As long as her husband treated her perfectly and provided everything that she wanted materially, she "forgave" him his infidelity. But inside she still harbored smoldering resentment. For years that mindset greatly affected her relationship with her husband.

Another forgiveness trap is suppressing anger. One man had supposedly forgiven his business partner for making a mistake in a business deal that cost the company thousands of dollars. But the man found himself taking out his anger and frustrations on his partner in little ways. It took years before he realized that, rather than completely forgiving him, he had forgiven only to a degree and for the most part had simply suppressed the rest of his anger.

A third trap is when we allow people to continue to hurt us. When we forgive another person, we must not harm him, just as a dove never attacks. But we must also exercise the wisdom of a serpent, which never places its head on the path where somebody is about to stomp with his boot. Serpents are shy creatures who avoid confrontation. When they are cornered they may attack out of self-defense, yet the normal nature of the serpent is simply to stay out of the way. The safest way to deal with snakes is to make enough noise as you approach that they have an opportunity to flee before you get close to them.

Nor does forgiveness mean condoning wrong. Rather, forgiveness presupposes that the issue has been dealt with. Does this mean we forget when we forgive? No. Our computerlike brains have an incredible capability for remembering, even though emotionally we sometimes block out painful things that have happened to us. The memory of painful experiences remains present, frequently existing in layer after layer.

So how do we forgive? We are to forgive before sunset, which was bedtime in the first century. However, sometimes we think we've thoroughly forgiven only to wake up the next day to persistent anger. Often forgiveness involves a commitment to the process of dealing with bitterness over and over again, whenever it flares up. It's a painful process, sometimes filled with tears and hurt. We forgive at great cost to ourselves. Yet the goal is to continue to deal with the issues until the emotional pain no longer exists.

In some situations that will take intensive counseling and require that we will to make difficult choices. But if we are to love people appropriately and unconditionally, we have to forgive them.

To choose to forgive, whether we feel like it or not, is an essential prerequisite for moving beyond burnout.

As we try to relate to others on the basis of unconditional love, however, we quickly find that forgiving isn't enough. We also have a strong need to develop positive relationships to which we can contribute and which will encourage and strengthen us.

Philip and Dick were college roommates who often played basketball together and double-dated together. After both graduated from college, they went their separate ways for five years without seeing one another. Yet each often thought of the other.

One spring, Philip's business took him to the Midwest where Dick was working. Certain about how he felt toward his old friend, but uncertain as to how he would be received, Philip decided to risk a phone call. Dick was ecstatic. The two men had lunch together, and Dick invited Philip to visit his family. As a result, both men verbalized their disappointment in themselves for allowing time and the pressures of life to erode their commitment to keep in contact.

Philip said, "Why don't you plan on bringing your family and spending some vacation time with us on the East Coast?" The two families spent a week together, and the ease with which the relationship was reestablished confirmed the genuine long-term commitment between Philip and Dick.

Have you ever been out of touch with old friends for years only to get back together and realize that the relationship is just as strong and solid as ever? If so, that friendship likely involved a long-term commitment. To verbalize such a commitment to a friend by saying, "I'm committed to you," "I care about you," or, "I'm with you for the long haul" is appropriate and provides tremendous encouragement, support, and hope for friends who are experiencing adversity.

LESSONS FROM PROVERBS

"A man of many friends comes to ruin, but there is a friend who sticks closer than a brother."[2] That proverb suggests that a lot of friends can be destructive, but a few good, close, loyal friends can help. An authentic friend is one who knows you at your best and worst and still loves and accepts you.

CONFRONTATION

Another proverb states that an open rebuke is "better . . . than hidden love. Wounds from a friend can be trusted, but an enemy multiplies kisses."[3] We need faithful friends—friends who can be trusted to tell us the truth. We may be tempted to surround ourselves with people who only flatter us, who only tell us what we want to hear. But a genuine friend is one who will tell us the truth even when it wounds us.

A friend was investing far too much time in work. Although many people said, "What you're doing is great," a few close friends said, "What you're doing is destructive. It ultimately will cause you to lose your health and the ability to work five or ten years down the road." Even though the words were painful, the man needed to hear them.

Appropriate confrontation is far better than a "Judas kiss." A true friend tells it like it is in contrast to the flatterer, who may cause us to stumble.

ENCOURAGEMENT

The book of Proverbs has a lot to say about the subject of encouragement counsel or direction. A true friend faithfully comforts as well as confronts. "Ointment and perfume rejoice the heart; so doth the sweetness of a man's friend by hearty counsel."[4]

The Hebrew people lived in a hot, dry climate. So oil on the skin provided a soothing, refreshing balm, and perfume stimulated the senses and encouraged appreciation for the finer things of life. So it is with the encouragement and comfort of a good friend. None of us can be "up" all the time. We all need counsel from the heart, the kind of encouragement a friend can give.

COUNSEL

Many people are unwilling to ask for advice. Others ask the wrong person or fail to heed good counsel. But we all need "hearty counsel" from time to time. The word used for *counsel* carries the idea of seeking direction. Most of us, when trying to find a place we've never been before, have needed to stop and ask for directions. The concept of seeking counsel is the same. Its root is related to a nautical word for a rope that is pulled to help steer a ship.

"For lack of guidance a nation falls, but many advisers make victory sure."[5] This context refers to people, relations, and activities within a city or community, although the advice can apply also to individuals. Security in each case comes from "a multitude of counselors." Ensuring safety or security necessitates skill in making decisions. The concept of utilizing many advisers carries the idea of our seeking a second opinion. We should not simply limit ourselves to the counsel of one friend or individual, just as we should not always depend upon the opinion of one physician. Perception and perspective are improved with two eyes rather than with only one. Similarly, it is far safer to utilize the perspective of two or more persons.

SUCCESSFUL PLANS

Another proverb gives a similar perspective: "Plans fail for lack of counsel, but with many advisers they succeed."[6] Here the issue is not simply safety but success and fulfillment in life. Without counsel, purposes will come to naught. We may plan as we wish, but we may experience disappointment if plans are made foolishly.

In the years following the oil bust in Texas, hundreds of new, empty office buildings in Dallas, Austin, and Houston lined the landscape. Each of those buildings represented plans and purposes that had been disappointed. Every week the newspapers carried column after column of bankruptcy declarations, many of well-known, previously wealthy people.

However, some individuals were able to maintain fiscal stability and success during that time. Such a man was Jim, a banker who had been involved in oil and real estate investments. He was advised by two individuals to diversify and to exercise caution before going into projects during the years when the oil decline first affected the economy. Because he listened to his advisers, Jim enjoyed a personal and financial stability not experienced by many of his peers. Counsel heeded led to success. Jim was a living example of the truth of this proverb: "Make plans by seeking advice; if you wage war, obtain guidance."[7]

"For waging war you need guidance, and for victory many advisers."[8] The context is strength and stability to face impending conflict or a developing war. Conflict is a common aspect of life; it often occurs among families, in business, among nations, and even in the church. The principle of that proverb applies not only to presidents, such as John F. Kennedy facing the Cuban missile crisis, Ronald Reagan dealing with Libyan leader Muammar Khadafy, or George Bush confronting Desert Storm, but also to us when we face conflict at home and at work. Those are the times we need wise counsel.

A church faced a major conflict over whether or not to build a new building. Even though the members had long agreed that a new building should be constructed, an offer for a different, free location for the new building created controversy. Some members saw the new location as a great opportunity, but others remained loyal to the church's location of the past thirty years. The conflict threatened to split the church. The pastor sought counsel from the elders in the church, from other experienced pastors in the area, and from church leaders in other parts of the country. After seeking a multitude of counselors, the pastor and the elders devised a plan for harmony. Ultimately, the plan worked to pull together the congregation. Those who stayed worked together and saw the new facility constructed. And the church's growth and its outreach in the community continued in an even larger measure.

Everyone needs friends from whom he can seek open counsel —friends who will give him encouragement and friends he in turn can stimulate and sharpen.

MUTUAL INTERACTION

"As iron sharpens iron, so one man sharpens another."[9] That proverb gives a vivid image of mutual intellectual and spiritual interaction and growth among friends. Occasionally such interaction, like "iron sharpening iron," will cause sparks to fly. One of the best definitions we know for encouraging each other is: to comfort the afflicted or to afflict the comfortable. Encouraging one another can help all of us. Some people leave very little impact on our lives, whereas others, who encourage us, leave indelible impressions.

LOYALTY

Another important principle of friendship is loyalty. "Do not forsake your friend and the friend of your father, and do not go to your brother's house when disaster strikes you"[10] When adversity strikes, it's time to demonstrate loyalty to friends and to anticipate their loyalty toward us.

Tim was a section leader in a medium-sized corporation. He and Harold, his department manager, had worked together for a number of years. They had been employed by the company at the same time and had risen to management positions.

A new corporate vice president was hired with whom Harold did not see eye to eye, and Tim was offered Harold's job without Harold's knowing it. Because of his loyalty to his friend, Tim turned down the offer. He knew Harold was a good manager and that the complaints of incompetence that the new vice president voiced about Harold had no basis. Turning down the position, however, almost cost Tim his job.

Ultimately, Harold quit the company and moved to another. He and Tim remained good friends. Tim was not promoted into Harold's old spot but, as he told a friend, "My friendship with Harold was a lot more important than the promotion, especially with what I would have had to do to get it. I believe Harold would have stuck with me if the shoe were on the other foot. I couldn't have faced myself in the mirror if I had done that to him."

Loyalty can mean keeping issues between you and your friend without breaking confidences, or just giving appropriate encouragement or a proper word of rebuke. It includes verbally giving the right word of refreshment, without making promises that you cannot or will not fulfill.

But loyalty and close friendship don't mean we should presume on past times of intimacy. "If a man loudly blesses his neighbor early in the morning, it will be taken as a curse."[11] The principle communicated by this proverb is twofold: (1) practice sincerity in verbal communication and be sensitive to a friend's feelings, and (2) know when to back off. Even close, loyal friends may need some distance at times.

NOTES

1. Karl Menninger, *The Vital Balance* (New York: Viking, 1963), p. 94.
2. Proverbs 18:24. Except where noted otherwise, all Proverbs references are quoted from the *Holy Bible: New International Version.*
3. Proverbs 27:5-6.
4. Proverbs 27:9, King James Version.
5. Proverbs 11:14.
6. Proverbs 15:22.
7. Proverbs 20:18.
8. Proverbs 24:6.

9. Proverbs 27:17.
10. Proverbs 27:10
11. Proverbs 27:14.

17
HANDLING THE CIRCUMSTANCES OF LIFE

A young man, on the day of his college graduation, was asked, "What do you plan to do?"

"To succeed," he replied. A worthwhile goal, indeed, but one needing further definition before it could be achieved.

Our goals and objectives in life need to be broken down into specific subgoals. The overarching goal of being physically fit may include specific targets concerning weight control, proper eating habits, and exercise. The overarching goal of maintaining thriving interpersonal relationships may include a specific checklist having to do with developing friendships and spending time with one's spouse, children, and friends. The overarching goal of developing intellectual sharpness may include the subgoal of enrolling in academic courses plus embarking on a personal reading program.

Our goals need to be *attainable*. Unfortunately we tend to set our standards too high, particularly if we are perfectionists. Recently, a staff counselor at our clinic lost nearly fifty pounds within a year. For most of us, such a goal probably would not be attainable. We are often faced with a dilemma: what price are we willing to pay to achieve a specific goal, and will the achievement of our goal create imbalance in other areas of our lives?

Our goals need to be *measurable*. It is of little value simply to plan to achieve. Rather, you need to have a specific measure of both quantity and time. If you plan to jog twenty minutes three times a week throughout the next year, you will know whether or not you are fulfilling your goal.

Our goals need to be *flexible*. That is particularly true for the obsessive-compulsive. It is easy for us to become so committed to a specific goal that we feel like a total failure if we fail to reach that goal. Even worse, in the process of trying to meet one goal we may neglect other basic needs, either our own or the needs of those around us. Occasional mid-course corrections have been necessary of every manned venture into space; similar corrections need to be incorporated into our lives as well.

We must remember that growth is *not instant*. A few years ago one of the authors and his family moved into a house in a suburban community north of Dallas. In that subdivision houses were stacked row upon row. Each house had two "instant trees" planted in the front yard. Within the first three months these instant trees had to be replaced twice. However, in the backyard was a massive pecan tree that obviously had been around long before the subdivision. Many years before, a pecan had fallen to the ground and taken root, and from it sprouted a small, fragile tree that grew and withstood the elements. It drew nutrients from the soil, carbon dioxide from the air, and energy from the sunshine. Today it furnishes shelter, shade, beauty, and even the makings of an occasional pecan pie—all because it was allowed time to grow.

OUR IMMEDIATE PRIORITIES

What are some priorities of growth that we need to recognize as immediate needs?

CHARACTER DEVELOPMENT

Many people today emphasize excellence only in what they do. Instead we should focuses more on character—what we *are*. Over an extended period of time former Dallas Cowboys head coach Tom Landry has exhibited excellence of character. For most of that time his Dallas Cowboys succeeded, but there were times they did not. It was evident that Tom Landry was a man who exhibited excellence, not simply in achievement but also in character.

OUR USE OF TIME

The idea of redeeming the time, a phrase that literally means "to buy back," involves freeing our time. It is not simply packing life with more activity. Rather, it necessitates developing balance in our lives so that we can utilize opportunities that come our way.

There is so much we want to do, so much that needs to be done, and so much that society insists we must do. As one O-C housewife put it, "We must not have ring around the collar. We must have floors that gleam until we can see our faces in them. We must have furniture that reflects an arranged bouquet in living color. We must be gourmet cooks, publicly aware, socially active, and academically and intellectually current. And on top of all that, succeed as wives and mothers and perhaps in an additional career as well."

Our obsessive minds can easily operate on a strictly scheduled basis, but we need to allow ourselves to incorporate opportunity. In *How to Have All the Time You Need Every Day*, Pat King says of interruptions, "When we drop our list and change our plans for [God's] work . . . He more than makes up for the time given."[1] She goes on to observe that from her experience almost everything on her list winds up being accomplished eventually anyway.

HANDLING ADVERSITY

How we determine our priorities is frequently reflected in how we deal with adversity. One test is what we do when we lose possessions. With many obsessive-compulsives, maintaining hold of possessions is mandatory. That is because we often have the wrong perspective on success. We view success as determined by what car we drive or how we look. Many of us have a dress-for-success mentality. Webster defines success as "the attainment of wealth, favor, or eminence." Michael Corda, in his book *Power! How to Get It, How to Use It*, says, "All life is a game of power. The object of the game is simple enough—to know what you want and get it."[2]

Our society places a strong emphasis on "getting." We are consumers geared toward the lust of the flesh, often overeating and harming ourselves. We also have become caught up in the lust of the eyes, going on shopping sprees, waving our plastic credit cards, grabbing far more than we ever need. We become entrapped in the pride of life, proud of our designer clothes, our carefully manicured hands, or our landscaped lawns. Yet, all those things are temporal.

Certainly it is appropriate for us to enjoy our possessions. We can enjoy the world without loving it. We are to be content to have our basic life needs met, but at the same time we must avoid the temptation and harmful consequences of the overwhelming desire to be rich. We should flee coveting material possessions and pursue virtuous character. Though it is easy to have a "go for it" mentality regarding possessions, our focus should be on the next life.

The obsession to acquire money can be a major problem for many obsessive-compulsives. Sadly, rather than bringing security, the love of money is likely instead to lead to burnout. We should not trust in material possessions. Moving beyond burnout means having the right perspective on financial matters.

Stanley Marcus of Neiman-Marcus, in a *Dallas Morning News* column titled "Burnout: A Passing of the Buck," wrote, "Today psychological writing on burnout is everywhere." Marcus relates burnout to a "declaration of bankruptcy—something necessary but often irresponsible and undignified." He observes that the word *burnout* gained increased use in Texas during the oil-induced recession of the late 1980s. According to Marcus, blaming burnout allows us to pass the buck to other people and circumstances rather than forcing us to learn to overcome life's obstacles. In short, Marcus suggests, we need to exercise responsibility before burnout occurs.[3]

NUMBERING OUR DAYS

After years of successfully managing the New York Yankees, Dick Howser reached the pinnacle of his managerial career in 1985 when he led the Kansas City Royals to a dramatic seventh-game World Series victory. A man of small stature yet boundless energy, Howser had seemingly reached the top.

The following year he led the American League All Stars to a 3 to 2 victory over the National League squad. Although no one knew it at the time, that was to be Dick Howser's last appearance as a major league manager. Shortly afterward he complained of serious pain and was hospitalized. Surgery revealed a malignant brain tumor. Although Howser attempted a comeback, he eventually announced his resignation just before the start of the 1987 season. During the long months of struggling against his debilitating illness, he did not allow the prospect of death to defeat him.

Less than eleven months after reaching the pinnacle of his career, Dick Howser died June 17, 1987. The next day, *Kansas City Star* sports writer Gib Twyman described him as a man who focused "on the positive, the upbeat, a high note as high as heaven itself." Twyman quoted Howser as saying, "God has already told me I'm going to heaven. I know I'm going to be happy."

What gave Dick Howser victory over death? He had learned to number his days and apply his heart to wisdom. For Dick Howser —as for us—to "number our days" involved acknowledging his need of meaning and purpose in this life as well as beyond his earthly existence. Dick "applied his heart to wisdom" by personally trusting Jesus Christ for forgiveness, meaning, and security. For Dick Howser, life—even in the face of death—made sense because of personal trust.

All of us will eventually face death. If we, like Dick Howser, are to have victory over death, we also must learn to number our days and apply our hearts to wisdom. Numbering our days will give us a legacy that outlives this present life. Our lives, properly invested, can produce lasting fruitfulness.

During the summer of 1987 a number of men met with James Dobson and other members of "Focus on the Family" radio show at El Canyon Ranch in Montana for a week-long retreat of planning and mutual encouragement. After the retreat, four men from Dallas boarded a twin-engine Cessna 421 to return home. They never made it.

Three days later, rescue workers found the bodies in the wrecked aircraft in a treeless area of the Shoshone National Forest fifteen miles west of Kote, Wyoming. The impact of the deaths of those men jolted the Dallas-Fort Worth area. Local media provided extensive coverage. Thousands gathered to pay tribute at a joint memorial service at which Dr. Dobson gave an eternal perspective:

> Would you not have enjoyed being there when these men made the transition to the other side? The Lord greeted them and wrapped His arms around them. Creath was laughing. I know he was. And Hugo was talking in that Texas accent that most of us couldn't understand very well. Knowing them as I did, I can hear them saying, "But Lord, what about our families?" And I know the Lord gave them the assurance that He is going to be with you all—and He will. . . . Your fathers are alive, and we will see them again some day.[4]

They were men whose lives had made incredible impacts; yet their deaths made equally great impacts.

THE BOTTOM LINE

- *I am not isolated from God.*

For many years the football field at the University of Alabama was dominated by a twenty-foot tower. Brian Newman, a therapist at our clinic and an Alabama alumnus, remembers that tower as the place where legendary coach Paul "Bear" Bryant spent the hours of football practice. While his assistants worked with the offense, defense, and special teams, Coach Bryant carefully observed from his tower. He always knew what was happening; he knew when the players were doing well and when they were not. In similar fashion, God sees and knows every facet of our every experience. We can take comfort in the fact that nothing escapes His scrutiny.

- *Circumstances discipline us.*

One of the authors played football in high school. His first two weeks of summer practice under the hot sun were an unforgiving introduction to the world of athletic conditioning. One session of leg lifts seemed especially brutal. The coach quietly encouraged the players, "Think of the good things in life." To which one of the players replied, "There aren't any." The coach said, "Sure there are. In a couple of weeks you'll be able to do this with no pain." Sure enough, two weeks later the coach's prediction proved to be correct.

- *There is a process that refines us and improves our character.*

Sometimes adversity simply happens. When it does, we need to have the appropriate attitude. Thankfulness should be a significant portion of that attitude.

Thankfulness is therapeutic. Many times the authors of this book have recommended that individuals who feel overwhelmed by their problems make a list of the positive things for which they are thankful. We have also recommended that they maintain a "blessing" journal as a long-term project and regularly review the benefits cataloged in that journal.

We need to encourage and motivate thankfulness in others. Our disposition affects both our own well-being and the well-being of those around us.

Another significant element of attitude is a positive spirit. A "merry heart" from the book of Proverbs is not the mirth of modern comedians or fools. The idea of *merry* means "joyful" or "good" in the sense of "pleasant" or "happy." This component of our personality can have a strong influence on others, for the condition of the heart leaves its stamp on the appearance and the activity of an individual.

A merry heart produces a pleasant countenance. This pleasant countenance can in turn lead to a festive outlook on life. A person may spend each evening eating at upscale restaurants, yet feel miserable. Another person, however, may be able to look at a trip to Mc-Donald's as the ultimate in happy eating experiences.

In addition, a merry heart can actually produce good health. Psychiatric research has noted that more than 50 percent of all hospital beds have a significant emotional component in the diagnosis of the patients who occupy them. Why? Because the emotional affects the physical, and the spiritual can affect both. Yet so often we allow the circumstances of life to crush our spirits. The concepts of a merry heart and good health both appear within the context of sickness. Developing a merry heart and encouraging it in others can help us avoid illness and lead to good health.

It is also important, especially for Type A's and perfectionists, to balance the long and short views of circumstances. One of the contrasts we have examined is between the quantity-oriented Type A and the quality-oriented perfectionist. The Type A often tends to jump into too many tasks and develop that as a style of relating. Often he does not think of the long-term consequences of such decisions.

Mike, a typical obsessive-compulsive businessman, was offered a new position with his company, plus a substantial increase in pay. Without consulting anyone for advice or input—or even discussing the matter with his wife or family—Mike made his decision. Soon the moving van arrived and Mike's family and belongings were transported to a new home thousands of miles away.

Sadly, however, Mike hadn't considered the long-term consequences of his decision. His wife became depressed because she lacked friends. The children began acting out in school in response to the trauma of being uprooted. Mike soon ran into conflicts in his new job responsibilities. The result was devastating. Mike needed to develop a long view to better visualize the long-term consequences of his decision, either in counseling or simply by working through the issues himself.

On the other hand, the perfectionistic obsessive-compulsive needs to develop the short view. These people will often refuse to make a short-term decision or to take action immediately because they are so fearful of being overwhelmed by the long-term consequences of present actions.

Janice had just graduated from college with a degree in teaching. She was all set to become a skilled teacher. She was given three or four opportunities, but she wound up letting deadlines pass on all of them. Instead she took a job as a grocery store checker. Janice was afraid that whatever decision she made would unalterably commit her to that particular job, with its strengths and weaknesses.

The O-C somehow needs to achieve balance, and, as in these examples, balance can be observed in attitude. Type A tends to have a "go for it" mentality but sometimes tends to give up and become discouraged. The perfectionist will tend to fear "going for it" but will "keep on keeping on." There is a time to go for it, and there is a time to keep on keeping on. Both the fearful perfectionist and the gung ho Type A compulsives need to recognize that they can learn from each other.

TYING UP THE PACKAGE

Some time ago, a young man named Bruce came rushing into the office of one of the authors, an almost frantic look on his face. He had the appearance of success about him, from the neat razor-cut of his hair to the sole of his well-shined wingtips. His countenance reflected the stress factor so common to many of his generation.

"I'm stressed out," he said almost before settling into the chair he was offered. "And I need bottom-line answers. Maybe there's a medication you can recommend—a tranquilizer perhaps. Or, if not, perhaps some profound truth that will somehow cut my stresses to manageable level. I just don't see how I can go on, the way things are."

Having learned from experience the danger of responding to a matter before hearing it out, and recognizing the ineffectiveness of "quick fix" answers to complex problems, we began asking questions to gently probe the depth and nature of the stresses that were pulling at the fabric of Bruce's life.

It turned out there were a number of factors—both major and minor—that were contributing to the unacceptable level of stress in Bruce's current experience. Three years before, he had lost his position as CEO of a small but rapidly growing service company. The job he had subsequently been able to obtain produced less than half the income he and his family had previously enjoyed. The resulting financial pressures had forced his wife to return to work—something she seemed to subtly resent. That further complicated an already shaky marriage relationship. Adding to those pressures was the fall-out from a sixteen-year-old son's drug and alcohol involvement.

Those major life stresses were complicated by a series of recent stressful events that could have been labeled minor, but in reality weren't. For example, Bruce had just wiped out his entire savings account to have the transmission of his wife's car repaired. In addition, he was looking at a significant outlay for counseling and help for his son. Furthermore, several items around the house needed repair—and Bruce suggested that his wife didn't hesitate to let him know about the inconvenience those plumbing and appliance problems were causing her. Even the family dog needed veterinary attention.

Reluctantly Bruce accepted our insistence that there were no quick solutions to his problems. He agreed to undergo a careful evaluation, which determined there were no serious medical problems other than stress-related hypertension. We then scheduled a series of therapy sessions designed to help Bruce deal with the stress factors in his life.

During the initial session, we learned that Bruce was the oldest in a family of four. Furthermore, he had been given, and had sought to fulfill, the role of "family hero" in a home in which both addiction and abuse had played a prominent role. From baby-sitting his younger siblings to earning success in the classroom and on the athletic field, Bruce had always been expected to be an achiever—and he had fulfilled the expectations of his parents and others in great measure.

Bruce had continued that pattern of success in his marriage and family, and in business—but ultimately at a great price. The stresses had led to burnout, a mid-life crisis, and deteriorating marriage and family relationships.

Bruce admitted that he felt exhausted most of the time—but he had trouble sleeping. We explained how the emotional exhaustion of burnout was quite different from the pleasant, healthy exhaustion felt after a vigorous workout. Bruce nodded, understanding. "That's exactly how I feel," he said. "Emotionally drained, used up."

Without prompting, he verbalized his experience of the other two components of burnout. "People irritate me—I can't get along with my family. The people I work with bug me. I don't enjoy getting together with friends anymore. I'd just like to make the world go away."

Later in the interview Bruce conceded he was "working harder and harder, but getting less and less done. I feel like I'm just spinning my wheels much of the time."

It didn't take long to catalog the stresses in Bruce's life, both major and minor. But it was a bit more difficult to get Bruce to see how his own perfectionism and drivenness played into his stressed-out experience. Using the denial typical of most workaholics, Bruce contended, "I don't consider myself a workaholic. My wife bugs me about it occasionally—but my boss sometimes suggests I don't work hard enough. He puts in seventy hours a week, but I usually limit myself to fifty or sixty."

Gentle but direct questioning brought Bruce to the admission that he frequently took projects home from the office, working into the night and on weekends. Actually his work time ran closer to between seventy and eighty hours per week—and that didn't include civic and church activities, which demanded even more hours. A time inventory brought Bruce to the realization that he was attempting to get by on six hours or sleep a night much of the time. No wonder he was, in his wife's words, "a walking time bomb around the family."

After several sessions helped Bruce begin to gain insight into his perfectionistic, workaholic, and Type A traits, another breakthrough occurred when he acknowledged how burnout's hidden root had affected him. His voice shaking with emotion, Bruce admitted, "I always thought I had no negative feelings toward my parents—in fact, I felt my childhood was ideal. I even denied the abuses my brothers and sisters were dealing with in their counseling. I can't get away from it now. I have to admit, I've been really angry toward both Mom and Dad. In fact, to be honest, I've been bitter. I never saw it as bitterness, but it is. I was holding a grudge toward them—in fact, I think, in a sense my 'mid-life crisis' was a futile attempt to get even with them for pushing me so relentlessly to succeed."

It was at this point that Bruce's counseling began to take a strong positive turn. Through diet, exercise, and proper rest, he began to recover physically from the debilitating effects of stress that, if left unchecked, could have literally killed him.

Emotionally, he became far healthier as he learned to deal with anger rather than stuff it away, as had been his pattern in the past. At the suggestion of his counselor, Bruce developed a network of men who became his close friends, his confidants, and a valued resource for sharing emotions such as anger, fear, or discouragement. Bruce also learned new and effective interpersonal communications techniques, which strengthened his relationship with his wife and his children. That in turn had a positive effect on his son, who was undergoing treatment for his drug and alcohol problem.

Spiritually, Bruce was able to move from a driven, legalistic approach to his faith to the point where he, in his own words, "Actually began to enjoy God for the first time in my life. I'd always viewed God like my dad—cold, isolated, ready to 'lay it on me' whenever I slipped up in the least possible way. Now I realize just how far off base that view of God was."

In his final session, we talked with Bruce about two important factors in his life: balance and serenity. After we discussed the competing demands of work, home, self, and others, Bruce pledged to continue to seek balance—and to request feedback from his wife as well as his new network of friends regarding any new areas of imbalance that might crop in the future.

Toward the end of the session we contrasted the serenity prayer,

> God grant me the serenity
> To accept the things I cannot change,
> The courage to change the things I can,
> And the wisdom to know the difference.

with the workaholic's prayer we had talked about earlier:

> Lord, help me get everything done.
> Now, please, and in order.

With the insight he had gained during the previous weeks, Bruce was able to laugh at the difference between those two approaches to spirituality. And it was evident to us as we concluded the interview that, although Bruce had come to us reflecting the workaholic's prayer, he was leaving with the perspective of the serenity prayer.

We've been extremely gratified to see literally hundreds of men and women like Bruce achieve balance and serenity as they've brought the stress factor in their lives under control. It is our hope that *The Stress Factor* can bring about this same result in your life.

NOTES

1. Pat King, *How to Have All the Time You Need Every Day* (Wheaton, Ill.: Tyndale, 1980), p. 49.
2. Michael Corda, *Power! How to Get It, How to Use It* (New York: Random House, 1986), p. 3.
3. "Burnout: A Passing of the Buck," *Dallas Morning News*, June 23, 1987.
4. James Dobson, *Focus on the Family*, September 1987.

GLOSSARY

ACTING-OUT

This term describes how some individuals use action as a response to unconscious conflicts. Often instead of responding to insight, a person relieves the repressed emotions by undertaking some kind of behavior, which is usually aggressive, antisocial, or otherwise inappropriate. For example, a young lady who has repressed anger toward her father may act out that anger by becoming sexually promiscuous; or a man with unconscious hostility toward his father may become physically aggressive toward his boss.

BURNOUT

A cluster of symptoms, including emotional exhaustion, depersonalization, or a desire to withdraw from people, and reduced accomplishment (working harder and harder while accomplishing less and less). Although current stresses contribute to burnout, other significant factors include obsessive-compulsive or perfectionistic personality traits and bitterness or unresolved anger.

COMPULSION

A seemingly irresistible urge to carry out an action or ritual series of actions. Closely related to obsession, the anxiety that leads to the compulsion stems from ideas or obsessions that may be unacceptable to the individual but nonetheless force their way into conscious awareness. The compulsion displaces attention from the obsessions, thus relieving anxiety. Common compulsions include checking and rechecking locks, or repeated handwashing.

CONFLICT

The presence of divergent goals or aims within an individual, between two individuals, or within a group. Internal conflict may involve such competing feelings as the need for autonomy versus the need to be dependent on a partner, or a highly positive, idealistic view of self conflicting with a despising attitude toward self. One kind of conflict is termed approach-approach, when a person is attracted toward two desirable but mutually-exclusive goals. Also common is approach-avoidance conflict, where a strong attraction (purchasing a beautiful new home) may be balanced by a strong aversion (increased indebtedness). Conflict between individuals is frequently intensified when one individual wishes to cooperate while the other views the situation as competitive. The ability to function is usually improved as conflict is reduced.

CYCLOTHYMIC

The cyclothymic personality tends to experience intense ups and downs. Such individuals may feel highly elated for a period of time, then experience a period of deep depression. When high, a cyclothymic person is generally cheerful, humorous, and outgoing, though sometimes anger or sarcasm surface. In the depressed stage the same individual may appear sad, hopeless, helpless, despondent, or unable to perform. Periods of highs and lows may fluctuate rapidly, or they may persist over an extended period of time. Some individuals may spend the majority of their time in a depressed state, whereas others may tend to remain in the energetic high. Some individuals exhibit high energy and high achievement most of their lives and may be referred to as having "hypomanic" personalities.

HYSTERIC OR HISTRIONIC

A cluster of personality traits including a tendency toward immaturity, feelings that are intensely expressed but shallow, difficulty with interpersonal relationships, and an inclination toward the over-dramatic. The Diagnostic Manual DSM III-R uses the term *histrionic*, which is derived from the Latin term for actor, *histrio*. Individuals with such personality traits may be charming and socially active, yet they also have difficulty with deep or intimate relationships. They may be demanding and manipulative. Frequently internal sexual conflict, such as unresolved anger with the parent of the opposite sex, may be present. The terms *hysteric* and *histrionic* are often used interchangeably.

OBSESSION

A persistently recurring thought or feeling, usually involuntary and inconsistent with the individual's conscious character. Obsessions usually originate in conscious attempts to deny certain unconscious desires or anxieties. Often an obsession will lead to a consuming preoccupation with philosophical or theological questions such as whether the individual has committed the unpardonable sin. Obsessions generally lead to compulsions.

OBSESSIVE-COMPULSIVE

Individuals with this particular cluster of personality traits tend to be conscientious, self-sacrificing, organized, perfectionistic, and devout. Such individuals are driven by repetitive persistent ideas or obsessions that intrude into conscious thought. Frequently their content is the opposite of what the individual would think voluntarily. Such obsessions lead to compulsions, or repetitive behaviors that are often performed ritualistically.

Obsessive-compulsive personality types commonly experience a wide range of difficulties, including perfectionism, Type A behavior, burnout, clinical depression, anxiety attacks or phobias, and even suicidal thinking. Drinking, gambling, sexual disorders or overeating are often classed as obsessive-compulsive behaviors. Obsessive-compulsive tendencies can be present in degrees ranging from mild to such severity that the life of the individual is disrupted. Gaining and acting on insight into the origin of the obsessions and compulsions can help the obsessive-compulsive personality strengthen his strengths while working on his weaknesses.

Those with intense obsessive-compulsive traits may gain help through appropriate psychiatric medications, since obsessions and compulsions are currently seen as an expression of the brain's tendency to form repetitive or circular response patterns when certain alarm responses are inadequately dampened. Medication can frequently eliminate these "short circuits," bringing important relief.

PARANOID

Individuals with paranoid personality traits tend to be suspicious, argumentative, hypersensitive, and jealous. Frequently they blame others for shortcomings and conflicts. Often the paranoid person is unreasonably jealous and may have delusions of persecution or of grandeur. Some individuals with a paranoid disorder may have an intense, unshakable system of grandiose or persecutory delusions in one area, yet may be remarkably logical and functional in other areas. Usually the paranoid individual feels an intense lack of self-worth, which has grown out of long-term stress, abuse, or rejection. An important aspect of the paranoid personality is inability or difficulty with personal trust.

PASSIVE-AGGRESSIVE PERSONALITY

Individuals with this cluster of personality traits handle underlying emotions such as anger with passive action, which tends to disrupt both work and relationships. A typical passive-aggressive individual tends to procrastinate, obstruct, forget, and dawdle, while denying that such behavior is in any way intentionally oppositional. Often this individual may be negative, sullen, pessimistic, disinterested, or stubborn. While obstructing those around them, such individuals often seem unaware of the effects of their behavior. Passive-aggressive personality traits are often a hostile response to prolonged or intense dependency. In some cases the strong dependency needs of the passive-aggressive personality may leave such individuals susceptible to substance abuse.

PERFECTIONIST

This individual frequently has a large number of obsessive-compulsive personality traits that remind him: (1) of the concept of the ideal or perfect and (2) that he, himself, utterly fails to measure up to perfection. Often we see in perfectionists a combination of obsessive-compulsive and passive-aggressive personality traits, as seen in the example of the college student who discards a carefully researched and laboriously typed paper because of one small typographical error near the end of the document.

PERSONALITY TRAITS

The term *personality* is one of the more abstract concepts in the English language. It originates from the classical Latin term *persona*, which described the mask an actor wore in a play. *Personality traits refer to specific characteristics in an individual which, when taken together, give substance to the personality and allow one to categorize generally the individual with others who have similar characteristics.* Personality traits are the concrete differences that make individuals unique but that also mark individuals as similar.

SCHIZOPHRENIA

A clinical disorder marked by a thorough disturbance of feeling, mood, and thought involving psychotic breaks with reality. Classical symptoms have been described as involving "4 A's": flat or inappropriate facial affect, loose associations, autism, and ambivalent features. Other symptoms may include delusions—beliefs held to be true in the face of solid evidence to the contrary—and hallucinations—hearing, seeing, or feeling things that are not present.

Schizophrenia generally occurs in about 8 to 10 of every 1,000 people. Treatment involves medication, psychotherapy, community support, and stress management.

SELF-TALK

The internal process by which we give ourselves feedback and messages on an ongoing basis. Self-talk can be either negative or positive, accurate or inaccurate. Many individuals become conditioned to give themselves inaccurate, negative, and debilitating messages that are destructive in nature. Such negative self-talk often incorporates such distorted thinking as:

Magnification: "This is a terrible, horrible disaster!"
Selective attention: "This single low test grade outweighs all my other positive scores put together."
Personalization: "He's rejecting me. I must be a terrible failure."
Polarized thinking: "I have to be either totally good, or I'm totally bad."
Overgeneralization: "I can never do anything right. Locking my keys in the car today just proves it."

Insight into the underlying reasons for our negative self-talk (such as parental conditioning) coupled with cognitive restructuring can help turn self-talk into a positive tool rather than a negative habit.

STRESS

The word *stress* comes from a Latin term *strictus,* which means to be drawn tight. This concept from physics has to do with the measurement of weight strain on materials and mechanics that's used of the internal strength of metal, its ability to withstand pressure. Hans Selye wrote the classic *The Stress of Life* and talked about fight or flight as the "general adaptation system."

Dr. Selye divided people into two categories. Some of us are what he called race horses, the Type A, who thrive on a fast-paced lifestyle. Competitive-aggressive, highly motivated. Others would be more accurately described as turtles, moving slowly, practicing caution, needing peace and quiet rather than adventure and danger.

Cardiologists Meier, Friedman, and R. H. Roseman in the book *Type A Behavior and Your Heart* characterized Type A people as being prone to "excessive impatience, focused in insecurity . . . often with free-floating hostility." According to Friedman and Roseman, approximately 50 percent of people in America have quite a few type A traits. Type A is much more competitive, the Type B less competitive. Some people, perhaps 10 percent of the population, are a combination of the two.

TYPE A

Commonly associated with the obsessive-compulsive personality, Type A generally refers to a cluster of traits representing a person of high energy and intense activity. Type A personalities are prone to cardiac and other health risks; sometimes they are described as having "hurry sickness."

Coupled with the tendency to rush through almost everything in life, Type A's frequently exhibit symptoms of underlying anger. The combination of those stress-inducing tendencies make Type A's a high risk for burnout.

If you are interested in more information
about how to integrate principles from the Bible
with the subject matter of this book, please write
to the following address:

Northfield Publishing
215 West Locust Street
Chicago, IL 60610